T5-CFT-484

RETHINKING THE UNITY OF LUKE AND ACTS

MIKEAL C. PARSONS
AND
RICHARD I. PERVO

Fortress Press   Minneapolis

BS
2589
.P37
1993

RETHINKING THE UNITY OF LUKE AND ACTS

Copyright © 1993 Augsburg Fortress. All rights reserved. Except for brief quotations in critical articles or reviews, no part of this book may be reproduced in any manner without prior written permission from the publisher. Write to: Permissions, Augsburg Fortress, 426 S. Fifth St., Box 1209, Minneapolis, MN 55440.

Scripture quotations, unless otherwise noted, are from the New Revised Standard Version of the Bible, copyright © 1989 by the Division of Christian Education of the National Council of the Churches of Christ in the United States of America.

Cover design and illustration: *Ann Elliot Artz Hadland*
Interior design: *The HK Scriptorium, Inc.*

Library of Congress Cataloging-in-Publication Data

Parsons, Mikeal Carl, 1957–
    Rethinking the unity of Luke and Acts / Mikeal C. Parsons and Richard I. Pervo.
        p.   cm.
    Includes bibliographical references and indexes.
    ISBN 0-8006-2750-4
    1. Bible. N.T. Luke — Criticism, interpretation, etc.   2. Bible. N.T. Acts — Criticism, interpretation, etc.   I. Pervo, Richard I. II. Title.
    BS2589.P37   1993
    226.4'06 — dc20   93-9758
                                                                                    CIP

The paper used in this publication meets the minimum requirements of American National Standard for Information Sciences — Permanence of Paper for Printed Library Materials, ANSI Z329.49-1984.   ∞

Manufactured in the U.S.A.   AF 1-2750

97   96   95   94   93   1   2   3   4   5   6   7   8   9   10

Contents

Preface

In many ways, this volume is an anomaly, and its genesis is an interesting story in itself. Two authors produce one book about one ancient author who produced two books. One author is an Episcopal priest teaching in an Episcopal seminary on Chicago's North shore; the other is a Baptist minister teaching in a Baptist university in the Southwest. We are both interested in the same part of the Christian canon, the Lukan writings, but we both have distinct perspectives about their interpretation and employ diverse methods in exploration of those texts. If the old quip is true that Henry Cadbury earned his doctorate by depriving Luke of his, then it is equally true that this project, which attempts to underscore the division between Luke and Acts, became the basis for a personal friendship between its two authors, previously known to each other only through their writings. How then did this book come about?

In the fall of 1988, Mikeal Parsons delivered a paper entitled, "The Unity of Luke-Acts: Rethinking the *Opinio Communis*," to the Synoptic Gospels Section of the Society of Biblical Literature meeting in Chicago. Richard Pervo was in attendance at the meeting, approached Parsons after the session, expressed his appreciation, and asked for a copy of the paper. After several months of correspondence about the issues raised in the paper, it became clear to us both that the topic was worthy of a book-length treatment, and further, that the topic would benefit from our different perspectives, interests, and specialties. John Hollar, then Senior Editor of Fortress Press, gave his warm encouragement to proceed. Sporadic phone calls, occasional long letters, and time stolen at the annual SBL meetings over the next several years were supplemented by a visit of Pervo to the campus of Baylor University, where he presented the first draft of a paper which would eventually become chapter 4 of this book, "The Theological Unity of Luke and Acts." Although we both took major responsibility for drafting certain chapters (Parsons wrote the Preface, chapter 1, and chapter 3; Pervo composed chapters 2, 4, and 5), we each served as "first reader" of the other's writing, and the product is truly a co-authored work. The process has been stimulating and reinforced a conviction which we both shared from the beginning. Biblical studies has reached a point where it is often necessary for scholars to pool their resources and work together. Colleagues in the natural sciences have long been aware of the benefits of collaborative work—benefits which those working in the humanities are only now beginning to recognize.

In some respects, the argument of this book is rather modest. At a time when the unity of Luke and Acts is being stressed from many different quarters in the biblical guild, we hold that when scholars examine a broad range of generic, literary, and theological issues in Luke and Acts, they should do so without assuming unity as prima facie true. In spite of its simplicity, the implications of this argument are far-reaching and could alter the way scholars pursue questions about the genre, literary aspects, and theology of Luke and Acts. Monographs have been written on each of these topics (genre, narrative, and theology), and this book will thus only probe them in an exploratory way. At this point, it is more important for us to frame the questions than to attempt to settle these issues once and for all. We do hope that the methodological questions raised here will be taken seriously by others and will become the basis for some sustained reflection on and conversations about why and how Lukan scholars do what they do.

Many persons deserve our thanks. John Hollar was a source of much encouragement in the early stages and is sorely missed.

His request for a short book which might have a wider reader-ship is not only a wish we have sought to honor, but a desire the wisdom of which we now see much more clearly. His successor at Fortress, Marshall Johnson, has likewise given considerable support to the project. Robert Grant and Thomas H. Tobin, S.J., read portions of the manuscript with a critical eye. Alan Culpepper read the entire manuscript and made many helpful comments. Thanks also to Freda Virnau, Dennis Horton, and Robin Chance for preparing the indices. Tim Logan at Baylor's Computation Center was always ready to take Pervo's disks and convert them to a format compatible with Parsons's computer equipment. The University Lecturers, Research, and Sabbatical Committees of Baylor University have also been very generous in their support. William F. Cooper, Dean of Baylor's College of Arts and Sciences, provided Parsons with release time at a critical moment in the book's production. To all of these and others left unnamed we express our gratitude. Finally, we wish to dedicate this book, which in many ways is a review and critique of the history of Lukan scholarship, to those luminaries who have finished their journey: F. F. Bruce, Henry J. Cadbury, Hans Conzelmann, Ernst Haenchen, Colin Hemer, and John Knox. Εὐχαριστοῦμεν τῷ θεῷ πάντοτε περὶ πάντων ὑμῶν.

Abbreviations

AB	Anchor Bible
Adv. Marc.	Tertullian, *Adversus Marcionem*
AJT	*American Journal of Theology*
AnBib	Analecta Biblica
ATR	*Anglican Theological Review*
BETL	Bibliotheca ephemeridum theologicarum lovaniensium
Bib	*Biblica*
BTB	*Biblical Theology Bulletin*
CBQ	*Catholic Biblical Quarterly*
Cicero *Ad Fam.*	Cicero *Epistulae ad Familiares*
Cicero *De Leg.*	Cicero *De Legibus*
Cicero *De Nat. Deorum*	Cicero *De Natura Deorum*
Cicero *Resp.*	Cicero *Respublica*
Clement *Strom.*	Clement of Alexandria *Stromata*
1 Clem.	*1 Clement*
CTM	*Concordia Theological Monthly*
De Doctr. Christ.	Augustine of Hippo *De Doctrina Christiana*
De Exil.	Plutarch *De Exilio*
Diod. Sic.	Diodorus Siculus
Diss.	Epictetus *Discourses*
Ep. Mor.	Seneca *Epistulae Morales*
ExpTim	*The Expository Times*
Fr.	Musonius Rufus *Fragments*
GNS	Good News Studies
Hel.	Heliodorus

HTR	*Harvard Theological Review*
HTS	Harvard Theological Studies
ICC	International Critical Commentary
JBL	*Journal of Biblical Literature*
JosAs	*Joseph and Asenath*
JSNTSup	Journal for the Study of the New Testament, Supplement Series
JSPSup	Journal for the Study of the Pseudepigrapha, Supplement Series
JTS	*Journal of Theological Studies*
LEC	Library of Early Christianity
Nich Eth.	Aristotle *Nichomachaen Ethics*
NovT	*Novum Testamentum*
NovTSup	Novum Testamentum, Supplements
NTS	*New Testament Studies*
Orac.	*Sibylline Oracles*
Philo	
Conf. Ling.	Philo Judaeus *De Confusione Linguarum*
Philo *De Abrh.*	Philo Judaeus *De Abrahamo*
Philo *Dec.*	Philo Judaeus *De Decalogo*
Philo *Det.*	Philo Judaeus *Quod Deterius Potiori Insidiari Solet*
Philo *Praem.*	Philo Judaeus *De Praemiis et Poenis*
Philo *Spec. Leg.*	Philo Judaeus *De Specialibus Legibus*
Philo *Vit Mos.*	Philo Judaeus *De Vita Mosis*
Praescr.	*Praescriptio*
Protag	Plato *Protagoras*
PRS	*Perspectives in Religious Studies*
PTMS	Pittsburgh Theological Monograph Series
RAC	*Reallexikon für Antike und Christentum*
RESup	Supplement to *Realenzyklopädie der classischen Altertumswissenschaft*
RevExp	*Review and Expositor*
SBLBSNA	Society of Biblical Literature Biblical Scholarship in North America
SBLDS	Society of Biblical Literature Dissertation Series
SBLMS	Society of Biblical Literature Monograph Series
SBLSP	Society of Biblical Literature Seminar Papers
SBLTT	Society of Biblical Literature Texts and Translations
SUNT	Studien zur Umwelt des Neuen Testaments

SVF	*Stoicorum Veterum Fragmenta*
T. Abrh.	*Testament of Abraham*
T. Levi	*The Testament of Levi*
TDNT	*Theological Dictionary of the New Testament*
TF	*Theologische Forschung*
TRe	*Theologische Realenzyklopädie*
TRu	*Theologische Rundschau*
TS	*Theological Studies*
Xen Eph.	Xenophon of Ephesus

1

Introduction

THE UNITY OF LUKE AND ACTS
IN CRITICAL SCHOLARSHIP

Since the time of F. C. Baur, Luke and Acts have been in the forefront of scholarly debate, frequently, in van Unnik's oft-quoted phrase, "a storm center in contemporary scholarship."[1] This has not always been the case. Luke and Acts served different purposes in early patristic argumentation and exposition. Both Chrysostom and Jerome note a general neglect of Acts. Jerome observed that the Book of Acts was of no interest to his contemporaries because it presented only "unadorned history."[2] When Chrysostom delivered his Easter homilies on Acts in the year 401, he stated "To many persons this book is so little known, both it and its author, that they are not even aware there is such a book in existence."[3] In an earlier homily Chrysostom makes a kindred complaint at Antioch, where he calls Acts "a strange and new dish" and observes: "Certainly there are many to whom this book is not even known, and many again think it so plain that they slight it. Thus to some their ignorance, to others their knowledge is the cause of the neglect."[4]

---

[1] See W. C. van Unnik, "Luke-Acts, a Storm Center in Contemporary Scholarship."

[2] Jerome, *Epist. 53 ad Paulinum.*

[3] P. Schaff, ed., Chrysostom, *Homily* 1:1.

[4] P. Schaff, ed., *Homiliae in Principum Actorum,* iii, 54 (trans. mod.).

The recent notoriety of Acts, however, has not come without a price. Much of the popularity is due to the linking of Acts with its "better half," the Gospel of Luke. In fact, the presumed unity of Luke and Acts is axiomatic in current New Testament scholarship. For example, at the end of his exhaustive survey of Acts scholarship, W. Ward Gasque concluded:

> The primary gain of the recent criticism of Luke-Acts has been the recognition that the Gospel according to Luke and the Book of Acts are really two volumes of one work which must be considered together. Questions concerning purpose, theology, speeches, and historical value cannot be answered apart from a study of both volumes of Luke's two-volumed work.[5]

Robert Smith is even more forceful:

> That hyphenated label may seem inelegant or even barbarous, yet it is useful in the extreme; for it handily summarizes a hard-won position that is (or should be) a presupposition for all investigation of the Third Gospel and the Book of Acts: the entire work from Luke 1.1 to Acts 28.31 is a unified whole. The Gospel and Acts are not just two books chancing to derive from the same pen. They are part one and part two of a single book, and neither should be studied in isolation from the other.[6]

This common opinion needs little documentation. Although earlier commentators on Luke or Acts accepted the traditional view that both writings come from the same hand,[7] they did not pursue the implications of this perspective. Recent major commentaries on Luke, however, strongly assert that these writings are two volumes of the same work.[8] Marshall's comments are typical: "The Gospel of Luke is part of a two-volume work, and it is difficult to write a completely satisfactory or

[5] W. Ward Gasque, *Acts,* 309.

[6] Robert H. Smith, "The Theology of Acts," 527.

[7] Norman Geldenhuys, *Luke,* 15; Alfred Plummer, *Luke,* vi; see also xi–xvii; A. R. C. Leaney, *Luke,* 1.

[8] I. Howard Marshall, *Luke,* 29; Frederick W. Danker, *Jesus and the New Age,* xii; Joseph A. Fitzmyer, *Luke,* I:vii; Charles H. Talbert, *Reading Luke,* 5.

comprehensive introduction to one half of the whole work."[9]
Commentaries on Acts show a similar tendency.[10]

Most noteworthy among the myriad of scholars for whom the
unity of Luke-Acts is an "assured result" of modern scholarship
are those now employing social-scientific and narratological
methods.[11] *The Social World of Luke-Acts,* edited by J. Neyrey,
assumes unity without argument.[12] Joseph Tyson and Robert
Tannehill, whose works represent the shift of emphasis in Lukan
scholarship toward literary analysis, assert that Luke and Acts
are a literary whole.[13] This methodological shift has invigorated
the old proposal that these books are best designated as "Luke-
Acts."[14]

Henry Cadbury's 1927 book, *The Making of Luke-Acts,* is now
regarded as the debut of this hyphenated title. Donald Juel, for
example, remarks:

> Cadbury, a distinguished professor of New Testament at Harvard,
> insisted that the two volumes be interpreted as part of a common

[9] Marshall, *Luke,* 29.

[10] F. F. Bruce, *Acts,* 18; Ernst Haenchen, *Acts,* 98–99.

[11] In addition to English works, most French and German works also affirm
the unity of Luke and Acts. The hyphenated expression, however, seems
limited to English writings. To be sure, some French scholars may write about
"Luc-Actes," but most prefer something like the expression used in a collection of essays by Augustin George, *Études sur L'oeuvre de Luc.* In his Foreword,
George made clear what his title meant: "Toutes ces études portent sur 'l'oeuvre
de Luc', c'est-à-dire sur le troisième évangile et les Actes des apôtres. . . . les deux
ouvrages forment un ensemble nettement homogène par son vocabulaire, son
style, ses thèmes, la cohérence de sa pensée." (All of these studies deal with
"the work of Luke," i.e., with the Third Gospel and the Acts of the Apostles . . . the
two works constitute a unit that is tightly integrated by its vocabulary, its style,
its themes, and its coherence of thought). Likewise, many German studies refer
to *das lukanische Doppelwerk* (the bipartite Lukan opus) or *die lukanischen Schriften*
(the Lukan writings). Although the phrase, "Luke-Acts" (or some derivative of
it), is mostly confined to English, French and German writers agree with the
sentiment of the expression if not the specific terminology.

[12] Jerome Neyrey, ed. *The Social World of Luke-Acts.*

[13] Joseph B. Tyson, *The Death of Jesus in Luke-Acts,* 4; Robert C. Tannehill, *The
Narrative Unity of Luke-Acts.*

[14] Chapter 3 will examine the origins of this "literary turn" and its effects
on Lukan scholarship.

endeavor. His *The Making of Luke-Acts* is a classic, required reading for any serious student of the New Testament. Following his lead, recent Lukan scholarship has broken with centuries of tradition by reading the Gospel and Acts together. Cadbury's hyphenated "Luke-Acts" is employed as an indication that the two volumes must be read as an entity.[15]

Cadbury himself took credit for the term in the preface to the 1958 edition of *The Making of Luke-Acts:* "It may help the reader place this 1927 publication in past history to remind him how many other books in English since then ... have employed the convenient hyphenated expression 'Luke-Acts.'"[16] Interestingly, Cadbury began to use the phrase in a series of articles which appeared in *JBL* in 1925–1926, before the appearance of *The Making of Luke-Acts.*[17] The phrase must have occurred to Cadbury some time between the publication of "The Identity of the Editor of Luke and Acts: The Tradition," in *The Beginnings of Christianity,* Vol. II, first published in 1922, and June 1925, in the first of his modestly entitled "Lexical Notes."[18]

Cadbury was quite clear that he meant more by the term "Luke-Acts" than merely an affirmation of authorial unity:

> Even the recognition of the common authorship of Luke and Acts is not enough. They are not merely two independent writings from the same pen; they are a single continuous work. Acts is neither an appendix nor an afterthought. It is probably an integral part of the author's original plan and purpose.[19]

[15] Donald Juel, *Luke-Acts,* 2.

[16] Henry J. Cadbury, *The Making of Luke-Acts* (hereafter referred to as *Making*).

[17] See "Lexical Notes on Luke-Acts I," 214–217; "Lexical Notes on Luke-Acts. II. Recent Arguments for Medical Language," 190–209; "Lexical Notes on Luke-Acts. III. Luke's Interest in Lodging," 305–322.

[18] See "Lexical Notes on Luke-Acts I," 214–"at the present writing (June 1925 . . .)." Scholars are slightly in error, then, when they trace the origin of the term itself to *Making*.

[19] Cadbury, *Making,* 8–9. Cadbury is here obviously reacting against C. C. Torrey's assumption, "In relation to the Third Gospel, the Book of Acts was plainly an afterthought. When Luke wrote his brief prologue to the former treatise, he certainly did not have in mind the continuation which included his own personal experiences" (*The Composition and Date of Acts,* 68). Cadbury did not thereby assert complete unity. See, e.g., Chapter 2 on Generic Unity.

Despite this widespread consensus, some have questioned the unity of the Lukan writings. Martin Dibelius had cautioned against making too much of the unity of the two writings: "The literary type of the book [Acts] is unique in the New Testament. This opinion is valid even though the text forms the continuation of Luke's Gospel. We must not over-emphasize the importance of this homogeneity with the Gospel."[20] A. C. Clark challenged the authorial unity of Luke and Acts in 1933.[21] In an appendix to his commentary, Clark argues on linguistic and stylistic grounds that "the differences between Lk. and Acts were of such a kind that they could not be the work of the same author."[22] Conzelmann's well-known thesis of a three-stage salvation history in Luke-Acts argues, in fact, rather well for a distinction between stories of Luke (The Period of Israel and the Period of Jesus) and Acts (the Period of the Church). He asserts that "the two books of Luke both belong together and are separate, as a result on the one hand of the continuity of redemptive history and on the other of its divisions."[23]

Recent trends in narrative analysis itself have also prompted challenges to this critical consensus. In a 1989 article, James Dawsey cites the work of Tyson and Tannehill as representative of the position biblical narrative critics have taken regarding the unity of Luke-Acts and asks: "Is it right to move from an assumption of sequence to one of narrative unity?"[24] Stephen Moore has recently raised serious theoretical objections to the whole notion of the Gospels as unified narratives and mentions

---

[20] Martin Dibelius, *Studies in the Acts of the Apostles*, 2. Dibelius (and Bultmann) reflect the perspective that Cadbury sought to refute, although he does not name them or other representatives.

[21] Albert C. Clark, *The Acts of the Apostles*. Clark knew of Cadbury's work in debunking the Hobart-Harnack thesis that Luke used medical terminology through Cadbury's 1919 monograph (see Clark, *Acts*, 405–406), although Clark mentions neither *The Style and Literary Method of Luke* nor *Making*. Ward Gasque's observation (*Acts*, 129) that Clark's learned commentary is "an extremely eccentric piece of work" reflects the general view.

[22] Clark, *Acts*, 394. For an evaluation of Clark's evidence, see chapter 3.

[23] Hans Conzelmann, *The Theology of St. Luke*, 17.

[24] James Dawsey, "The Literary Unity of Luke-Acts," 49; see also chapter 3 below.

specifically the problematic of the unity of the Lukan writings.[25] Moore notes that the basis for this recent hesitation is Mikeal Parsons's 1985 dissertation and subsequent papers.[26] The co-author of this volume has also raised persistent questions about the assumption of unity.[27] Although the critical opinion is still very much intact, these initial probings have at least gained attention, and some scholars are, for various reasons, expressing more reserve about wholesale acceptance of the unity of Luke and Acts. For example, John Nolland, in his recent Word commentary on Luke, argues: "To say that we have part one and part two of a single work would, however, be an exaggeration and would do less than justice to the evident differences between the works."[28]

Still, despite these studies which intentionally or incidentally raise questions about various aspects of the unity of Luke and Acts, it is remarkable that in a twenty-year period of New Testament research which has witnessed a frontal assault on the entire historical-critical enterprise from the priority of Mark to the dominance of redaction criticism as the interpretive method in gospel studies, the notion of the unity of Luke-Acts has remained virtually unscathed. In fact, the position has been strengthened by the challenge to Markan priority and the

[25] Stephen Moore, *Literary Criticism and the Gospels;* see also idem, "Are the Gospels Unified Narratives?" 443–458.

[26] These earlier investigations in turn gave rise to the present study. See Mikeal C. Parsons, *The Departure of Jesus in Luke-Acts;* "The Unity of the Lukan Writings: Rethinking the *Opinio Communis,*" 29–53. Earlier versions of this paper were presented to the regional and national meetings of the Society of Biblical Literature in 1988.

[27] Richard Pervo's *Profit with Delight* briefly listed differences between Luke and Acts as the basis for investigating the genre of the latter separately (pp. 3–4). These arguments were developed in "Must Luke and Acts Be Treated as One Genre?" 309–316, and now, further expanded and refined, appear below as chapter 2. In *What Are They Saying About Acts?* 6–13, Mark Powell devotes several pages to the relationship between Luke and Acts, taking his lead from the work of Parsons and Pervo. These various probes have given the impetus to the publication of this present volume.

[28] John Nolland, *Luke 1–9:20,* xxxiii. See also R. Tannehill, *The Narrative Unity of Luke-Acts,* 2:5–8; David Gowler, *Host, Guest, Enemy, and Friend;* Steven Sheeley, *Narrative Asides.*

dethroning of redaction criticism. If Henry Cadbury did not coin the term "Luke-Acts," he certainly popularized it, and since 1927 the hyphen has become gradually more secure in Lukan scholarship, finally falling firmly into place during the last decade or so. Perhaps the time has come to re-open the debate.

NEW PERSPECTIVES ON THE UNITY
OF LUKE AND ACTS

Critical scholarship has used the phrase, "unity of Luke-Acts" in various ways. When scholars use this term, they are speaking (sometimes indiscriminately) about one or more of the following dimensions: (1) authorial unity; (2) canonical unity; (3) generic unity; (4) narrative unity; and (5) theological unity. These terms require further explanation. Since authorial unity has no serious challenges, this area will receive only a summary discussion.

Authorial Unity

The loneliness of Clark's dissenting voice is eloquent testimony to the fact that although the identity of the author is still debated,[29] almost all New Testament scholars agree on this point: Luke and Acts were written by the same person, whether Luke the physician or not, whether a Jew or a Gentile, whether from Antioch or Ephesus (or someplace else).[30] We agree that

---

[29] Fitzmyer (*Luke*, 1:35–53; and more recently *Luke the Theologian*, 1–26) has offered perhaps the most sustained and forceful argument in favor of traditional authorship, although the majority of scholars are still dissuaded. Even the view that Luke was a gentile Christian writing to gentile Christians, to which many scholars have adhered, is now much disputed. See especially Jacob Jervell, *Luke and the People of God;* David Tiede, *Promise and History in Luke-Acts.*

[30] The debate about the actual author tends to confuse the literary categories of actual author and implied author. In the case of Luke and Acts, the actual author is unknown. Whoever the actual writer was, the implied author of Luke and Acts is, in our language, a Christian who can assign to a leading character

a single writer, Lukas, composed these two works,[31] — but the implications of such an assertion on Lukan scholarship demands closer scrutiny.

Canonical Unity

Likewise, the canonical disunity of Luke and Acts is not a debatable point. In their canonical order, Luke and Acts do not form one continuous narrative; they are separated by John. In fact, according to all the evidence available to us, Luke and Acts never stood side-by-side in any canonical list.[32] The oldest copy of the *Tetraevangelium* (the fourfold Gospel), ms. p[45] (ca. 200 C.E.), also contains Acts, in the traditional order: Matthew, Mark, Luke, John, and Acts. In the so-called "Western" order, the two apostles are listed first (Matthew and John), followed by the two apostolic companions (Luke and Mark). Here Luke and Acts could easily have been placed together, but Mark stands between Luke and Acts.[33] Likewise, two other fourth-century lists, the so-called Cheltenham Canon and the stichometry of Codex Claromontanus place Luke last among the Gospels, but Acts comes after the Pauline Epistles in the former and at the end of the New Testament books in the case of the latter.[34] In some cases,

---

sentiments lacking appreciation of Torah-observance (Acts 15:10) and who interprets the Jewish Scriptures in an exclusively prophetic and messianic sense with the assumption that these writings are fulfilled in Christ, e.g., as an author who interprets Scripture as a Christian document. With this perspective one may contrast, for example, the implied and actual authors of Romans.

[31] The name "Lukas" distinguishes the implied author from the Gospel he produced, to which we shall refer as Luke. As noted above, the relationship between this implied author and the real, anonymous author is uncertain, and no judgments as to the identity of the real author should be inferred from this nomenclature.

[32] An observation confirmed by Cadbury (*Acts in History,* 144).

[33] See especially the principal witness to the "western text," Codex Bezae, (D). See also the comments on "canonical issues" in chapter 2, below.

[34] The Cheltenham Canon is an African list and is found in A. Souter, *The Text and Canon of the New Testament,* 212–213. On this evidence, see Cadbury,

cases, Acts was placed with the General Epistles (see ms. p[74]), far removed from the *Tetraevangelium*.[35] These variations indicate, at the least, a disinterest among early readers in preserving the "unity" of Luke and Acts.[36]

Those who wish to argue for Lukan unity have usually solved this difficulty of canonical separation in one of two ways. Some scholars have argued that the two works were divided at the time of canonization.[37] Manuscript data and content problems led to proposals that the conclusion of Luke and the beginning of Acts were later interpolations. Kirsopp Lake argued that the ascension narrative in Luke 24 had been added later when the two works were divided.[38] Amos Wilder and Hans Conzelmann supported this view, and Phillipe Menoud further suggested that both ascension accounts were interpolations added when the one-volume work of Luke-Acts was divided upon its acceptance into the canon.[39]

Acts in History, 144, 161–62, who comments:

> Perhaps the nearest we come to evidence that Luke and Acts were ever copied in juxtaposition is to be found in the fact that in Codex Bezae the name John (Greek Johannes) is spelled with one "n" regularly in these two books, but with two "n's" in Matthew, John and Mark. . . . It has been suggested that this is due to the fact that in an ancestor of Codex Bezae the same scribe copied these two books and that they were in such order that Luke came just before Acts (p. 162).

For further comments about this list, see chapter 2, n. 13.

[35] See Robert Wall's evaluation of the evidence in his article, "The Acts of the Apostles in Canonical Context." For an analysis which examines the canonical function of Acts, see Mikeal C. Parsons, "Canonical Criticism," 279–287.

[36] Cadbury (*Acts in History*, 143–144) notes the same evidence about the canonical disunity of Luke and Acts but does not seek there to account for the separation. Earlier (p. 139) he had commented that, in addition to the physical restriction in scrolls (which caused the author to arrange the material into parts of equal size), because of the tendency (both modern and ancient) to classify material by content, "it was natural that the Gospel of Luke should be associated with other Gospels both before and after the possibility arose of closer physical association of books of such size."

[37] This was the view of Cadbury, *Making*, 10.

[38] Kirsopp Lake, *Acts of the Apostles*, 5:3; cf. James Hardy's discussion of Acts 1:2, *Acts of the Apostles*, 3:256–261.

[39] Amos Wilder, "Variant Traditions of the Resurrection in Acts," 311; Hans Conzelmann, *Theology*, 94; Phillipe Menoud, "Remarques," 148–156. Menoud

This hypothesis has never gained a broad following, although as eminent a scholar as Joseph Fitzmyer does find the interpolation theory attractive.[40] Ernst Haenchen has argued forcefully against the supposition that Luke's work was originally one volume and was divided upon canonization:

> First, the works were not taken into the canon by an ecclesiastical authority able to ensure the simultaneous alteration of all existing copies; their acceptance was, rather, a long drawn-out process. Nowhere have any traces come to light of the hypothetical older book. Second, it was daring enough to provide the gospel with a sequel in the shape of a book on the apostolic age, but it is downright unthinkable that, instead of closing the gospel with the Resurrection and Ascension, Luke should prolong it until Paul's arrival in Rome; for him the life of Jesus was a self-contained epoch in the history of salvation, one distinct from the period which followed.[41]

One could add to Haenchen's argument the fact that the textual histories of the two writings are very distinct.[42] The complexity of the textual transmission of Acts, whatever it says about the relationship between the Alexandrian text and the much longer Western text, suggests that Luke and Acts have quite distinct histories of reception in the early church.[43]

---

eventually changed his mind and accepted the authenticity of the verses in question. See idem, "Pendant (Actes i 3)," 148–156.

[40] Joseph Fitzmyer ("The Ascension," 419) notes approvingly: "many commentators . . . consider it highly likely that these works existed at one time in an earlier form, to which Luke later added not only the infancy narrative and prologue, but even the secondary prologue of Acts 1.1-2 and the ending in Lk 24.50-53."

[41] Haenchen, *Acts*, 99. Here, of course, Haenchen is following Conzelmann's picture of salvation history. Robert Maddox (*Purpose of Luke-Acts*, 3) has noted that "there is no evidence for the existence of the alleged single volume, and no convincing occasion for its division and supersession has yet been suggested."

[42] For the various solutions to this crux interpretum, see Cadbury, *Acts in History*, 149–155. Cadbury himself is reluctant to commit to any particular theory and more importantly does not comment on the implications for disunity between Luke and Acts that the fact of two distinct transmission histories seems to demand.

[43] Cadbury (*Acts in History*, 139–160) recognizes the distinct subsequent histories of Luke and Acts, but accounts for this separation with the following reasoning (p. 139): "Fortunately our author had the judgment or foresight to

Others have recognized the weight of Haenchen's arguments and the lack of any manuscript evidence for the interpolation theory, and have argued that the single work was divided at the time of composition.[44] Donald Juel's comments are illustrative:

> Since writing in the first century was done on scrolls, and since a limit was imposed on the length of a scroll, longer works required division into discrete "volumes." Scholars have determined that the Gospel of Luke and the Acts would each fill a normal scroll. Though there is some disagreement, the simplest explanation for the separation of the two volumes is size. The short rededication to Theophilus and introduction to Acts, with some brief reference to the preceding volume, would have been required at the beginning of a new and separate scroll. The practice seems conventional. That means, however, that the two books should be viewed as two parts of one literary unit, despite their separation in the present canon of the New Testament.[45]

Such a solution does not take seriously the sense of an ending in Luke 24:50-53. It is obvious from a close literary reading of the text that Lukas has not simply run out of space, as Josephus indicates he did in volume one of *Against Apion*.[46] Rather, Lukas has carefully constructed his ending to provide a proper denouement to his gospel. That Lukas could have coincidentally reached the end of the scroll at the same time he closed his gospel is possible, but could hardly be taken as the primary reason for ending where he does. At any rate, Lukas, unlike Josephus, does not suggest that space is running out.[47]

---

make each of his two volumes somewhat self-sufficient, though in doing so he has perhaps prevented some modern readers from recognizing their fundamental unity." Of course, one must note the tension between this statement and Cadbury's earlier contention that Luke and Acts form "one continuous narrative."

[44] Theodore Zahn was the first to hold this view. See Aune, *The New Testament in Its Literary Environment*, 77.

[45] Juel, *Luke-Acts*, 12.

[46] The text of *Against Apion*, I.322–325, is cited in full below, pp. 61–62.

[47] This theory of the division of Luke and Acts as due to the material limitations of scroll production is purely hypothetical, the arid sands of the Middle East have yet to yield *any* NT scrolls. The question of scrolls and canonicity is also pursued in chapters 2 and 3.

Granting for a moment that these two writings were intended by the author to be read as one continuous story, the fact remains that we have no documentation that they were ever so read in the early church. The data point to just the opposite. That the two writings are not united in their canonical form is evidence that the first readers read them separately and either intentionally split a one-volume work into two to create these two books or passively introduced the individual books at different points in the canonical order. Rather than lamenting the canonical editors' botched job, one would do well to reflect on the significance of this evidence of such reader reception.

Brevard Childs has written lucidly about the effects of the canonization process on Luke and Acts. He admits that Luke's volumes were separated at some point, although he explicitly rejects the notion that the division occurred during canonization: "It seems far more probable that Luke was first assigned a canonical sanctity and only subsequently did Acts acquire a similar status."[48] He comments on the canonical effect of these two writings: "Luke became part of the fourfold Gospel collection and received its interpretation within the context of this corpus. Acts was assigned another position as bearer of the apostolic witness which was clearly distinguished from that of the evangelists."[49] Assuming the unity of Luke and Acts, then, probes behind the text to a "pre-canonical" form which may have never existed.[50] And one does not have to be a practicing canonical critic to be impressed with the implications of that fact.

[48] Brevard Childs, *The New Testament as Canon,* 236. Childs writes:
First, on the basis of the prologue to Luke's Gospel the case has been made for the original integrity of the Gospel as a separate entity. The second volume of the Acts was added later. Accordingly, the form of Luke's first volume as a Gospel did not derive from the later canonical decision to divide the work into two. At most the separation of the two books left its literary mark on the final section of the Gospel but did not determine the genre of the first volume. (p. 116)

[49] Ibid., 239. Childs further notes (ibid.) that "the canonical function of Acts was not determined by the order of its placement within the New Testament collection."

[50] See Maddox, *Purpose of Luke-Acts,* 4.

Frederick Danker once noted:

> Who can assess the impediments to the understanding of Luke's thought that were erected through canonical interposition of John's Gospel between the two sections of Luke's work? Centuries passed until Henry Cadbury finally cleared the way for perception of the distinctive literary features and their rationale in Luke-Acts.[51]

If the canonical shape of Luke and Acts is to be taken seriously as Childs insists, Danker's question may be paraphrased to Cadbury's followers in this way: Who can assess the impediments to understanding Luke's thought and the distinctive literary features of Luke and Acts that were erected when Henry Cadbury made "Luke-Acts"?

Generic Unity

Generic, narrative, and theological unity are more open to serious question. First, objections may be lodged against the assumption that Luke and Acts share the same genre. During the 1970s, Gospel genre was a burning issue.[52] In addition to several significant volumes which appeared, there was a SBL Gospel Genre Group in the early 70s. The cumulative effect was a mounting challenge to the Schmidt-Bultmann hypothesis of the literary uniqueness of the Gospels.

In general, two alternatives concerning Gospel genre have emerged:[53] (1) *Jewish pattern.* The Gospels took their generic conventions from the Jewish milieu and had parallels with the Old Testament or they were Christian midrashim patterned on the Jewish lectionary cycle.[54] (2) *Greco-Roman pattern.* The Gospels

---

[51] Frederick W. Danker, "Review," 143–144.

[52] Much of the material in this section has been taken from Mikeal C. Parsons, "Reading Talbert: New Perspectives on Luke and Acts," in Parsons and Tyson, eds., *Cadbury, Knox, and Talbert,* 160–164.

[53] Other alternatives will be explored in chapter 2. These options reflect the now discredited opposition of "Jewish" to "Hellenistic" in the discussion of NT backgrounds.

[54] Old Testament parallels were suggested by D. A. Baker, "Form and the

were influenced by the literary conventions of the Greco-Roman milieu. The second alternative is by far the more popular of the two and has led to several options with regard to the genre of Luke and Acts. Charles Talbert has suggested Luke-Acts fits one form of the ancient biographical genre. For Talbert, Luke-Acts is similar to the *a* (life of the founder) + *b* (story of the successors) pattern found in Diogenes' *Lives of Eminent Philosophers.* Acts then is a succession narrative which records the actions of the followers of Jesus, founder of the movement.[55] David Aune has recently argued that Luke-Acts belongs to the genre of Hellenistic general history, even though he places the other Gospels in the biographical mode.[56] A small group of scholars have associated Luke and/or Acts with ancient historical novels.[57]

Most genre critics assume that Luke and Acts are to be taken together. In fact, the assumption of the generic unity of Luke-Acts has led to Aune's double-edged appraisal. On the one hand, although he disagreed with Talbert's conclusions, Aune commended Talbert's proposal because it "has the merit of attempting to find an analogy in genre to Luke-Acts as a whole."[58] On the other hand, Aune is critical of Richard Pervo, the most notable exception to the assumption of the generic unity of Luke and Acts. Pervo argues that Acts employs the generic conventions of the ancient novel.[59] Aune insists that "Luke-Acts *must*

Gospels," 13–26; R. E. Brown, "Jesus and Elisha," 85–104; and George W. E. Nickelsburg, "The Genre and Function of the Markan Passion Narrative," 153–184. The liturgical origins of the Gospels were argued more thoroughly by P. Carrington, *The Primitive Christian Calendar;* M. D. Goulder, *Midrash and Lection in Matthew;* idem, *The Evangelists' Calendar: A Lectionary Explanation of the Development of Scripture;* and more recently, *Luke: A New Paradigm,* 2 vols. This theory is harshly criticized by Leon Morris, "The Gospels and the Jewish Lectionaries," 129–156.

[55] See Charles Talbert, *Literary Patterns, Theological Themes, and the Genre of Luke-Acts; What is a Gospel?* For a critique of Talbert's position, see Aune, *The New Testament in Its Literary Environment,* 79. More recently, see Talbert's essay, "Once Again: Gospel Genre."

[56] Aune, *The New Testament in Its Literary Environment,* 17–157.

[57] See Susan Praeder, "Luke-Acts and the Ancient Novel," 269–292; Pervo, *Profit.*

[58] Aune, *The New Testament in Literary Environment,* 79.

[59] See Pervo, *Profit,* and the arguments developed in chapter 4.

be treated as affiliated with *one* genre, but Pervo treats Acts in isolation."[60]

On what grounds does Aune argue that Luke and Acts must be taken together in genre studies? His argument is worth quoting in full:

> The Gospel of Luke and the Acts of the Apostles originally con-
> stituted a two-volume work by a single author. . . . By itself, Luke
> could (like Mark, Matthew, and John) be classified as a type of
> ancient biography. But Luke, though it might have circulated
> separately, was subordinated to a larger literary structure. Luke does
> not belong to a type of ancient biography for it belongs with Acts,
> and Acts cannot be forced into a biographical mold.[61]

After reading Aune's description of the generic features of Luke and Acts, however, one could turn Aune's statement on its head and apply it to his own proposal: Acts does not belong to a type of ancient history for it belongs with Luke, and Luke cannot be forced into a historiographical mode. Although both affirmed that genre studies must address the genre of Luke and Acts as a whole, Talbert's analysis favors the Gospel and argues for biography, whereas Aune's study favors Acts and argues for historiography. Again, both scholars evidently assume generic unity on the basis of authorial unity, subsuming one narrative under the other. Pervo is willing to separate the two volumes. At the time of his dissertation research, the floodgate to Lukan unity had not been flung open; thus he was not compelled to provide full justification for treating the two works separately. One purpose of this volume is to provide that further justification for this procedure.

Aune himself acknowledges that writers of antiquity could employ different genres. He admits that "neither history nor biography was constricted by static literary canons," and that "during the late Hellenistic period history and biography moved closer together."[62] Aune notes that a number of ancient writers

[60] Aune, *The New Testament in Its Literary Environment*, 80.
[61] Ibid., 77.
[62] Ibid., 30–31.

did produce works of both types.[63] Herodotus, Thucydides, and Xenophon have all been credited with writing both in biographical and historical genres. In fact, Xenophon treated the life of Agesilaus twice, biographically in *Agesilaus* and historically in *Hellenica* 3 – 6.[64]

That Lukas could have written in multiple genres seems plausible, perhaps even probable. Such a conclusion would address the difficulty of finding a genre both Luke and Acts fit, a problem which is usually resolved by forcing one to fit the pattern of the other. Further, it would also allow studies like those of Pervo and of Hemer[65] to receive evaluation on the basis of their specific arguments, rather than simply to be dismissed as treating Acts in isolation. Finally, however, it would require abandoning the a priori assumption of the generic unity of Luke and Acts.

Narrative Unity

In what ways may advances in biblical narratology inform our understanding of the narrative unity of Luke and Acts? As noted earlier, recent literary studies are largely responsible for the resurgence of Lukan unity. These New Testament examinations of narrative unity hit their stride just as secular literary critics began to argue for serious attention to the gaps, fissures, and discontinuities of narrative.[66] Charles Talbert recently observed in his review of Robert Tannehill's first volume of *Narrative Unity:* "Is it not ironic that as biblical scholars influenced by non-biblical literary criticism begin to emphasize the organic unity of the biblical texts, much recent literary criticism seems intent on denying the very organic unity of

---

[63] Ibid., 29–30.

[64] Ibid., 30.

[65] See Colin Hemer, *The Book of Acts in Its Historical Setting.*

[66] From Frank Kermode to Derrida, the emphasis is moving away from the view of the organic unity of the text.

literary texts that biblical scholars seek to affirm?"[67] What would it mean to treat each Lukan writing as a discrete, though inter-related narrative?

Theological Unity

Finally, how does one determine the theological unity of Luke-Acts? Most attempts to probe Lukan theology have employed the method of redaction criticism. This technique moves between two poles: the internal theological tendencies of the document and the external occasion which prompted its writing. It is commonplace now to argue that studies in Lukan theology must take both Luke and Acts into account, but there is no con-sensus whatsoever regarding the occasion(s) which produced these writings. In fact, some scholars are skeptical that there ever was such an entity as the "Lukan community."[68] Robert O'Toole's comments are typical: "All attempts to tie Luke-Acts to one community and to its concerns have failed. Therefore, this book assumes a more general interpretation of *Sitz im Leben* and refuses to limit the Lukan audience to any one given com-munity."[69] The result, however, is an implicit assumption on the part of the interpreter that Luke and Acts share at least a similar occasion.

More problematic is the position which assumes theological unity or consistency, but dates the two documents years apart.[70] Yet, the very attempts to separate these two writings chrono-logically are, in part at least, the result of the discomfort felt by readers who discover that the theological interests of Luke

[67] Talbert, review of Tannehill, 138.

[68] See the insightful article by Luke Timothy Johnson, "On Finding the Lukan Community: A Cautious Cautionary Essay," 87–100.

[69] O'Toole, *Unity,* 13.

[70] Some argue the two writings were written in close chronological prox-imity; others suggest a gap of twenty years or so; still others argue that Acts was written before Luke. See Pierson Parker, "The 'Former Treatise' & the Date of Acts," 52–58; C. S. C. Williams, "The Date of Luke-Acts," 283–284.

differ from, and at times are in conflict with, those of Acts. To be sure, scholars have demanded too much theological consistency from documents which represent ancient popular literature.[71] One should not, however, miss the point that those who date the documents years or even decades apart and thus argue for separate occasions while at the same time arguing for theological unity between the documents, are at cross-purposes.

One could, of course, employ a different method (a newer literary approach perhaps) which does not demand the positing of some occasion (as does redaction criticism). Still, the theological tensions between the two writings remain; the scholar then must turn to reasons other than external occasion to explain them. We are not arguing that there is *no* theological coherence between Luke and Acts, but rather we are raising the question as to the benefit of allowing the tensions first to be recognized, and then to be understood. Previous attempts to synthesize Lukan theology have often resulted in the suppression of discordant themes and the subordination of one document to the other, or in some cases, one part of the document to another.[72]

The following chapters examine the unity of Luke and Acts from the perspective of each of these three disputed points: generic, narrative, and theological unity. The assumption of authorial unity of the Lukan writings has led, in part, to the conclusion that Luke and Acts are unified in these other ways as well. We seek to demonstrate that the unity of "Luke-Acts" is a largely unexamined hypothesis, and that upon closer scrutiny it may be more helpful to speak of Luke *and* Acts — a gospel and its sequel written by the same real author, but two very distinct narratives embodying different literary devices, generic conventions, and perhaps even theological concerns.

[71] See chapter 4.

[72] In order to synthesize Lukas's theological portrait of the Pharisees, scholars often subordinate the evidence of Luke to Acts or vice versa. See the comments to this effect by David Gowler, *Host, Guest, Enemy, and Friend*, 3–8. Also, the speeches in Acts are often given priority over the narrative materials in reconstructing Lukan theology. See, e.g., Dibelius, Cadbury, etc.

This is more of a programmatic than a substantial enterprise, a study intended to raise more questions than it attempts to answer.

Conclusion

At the end of the first chapter of *The Making of Luke-Acts*, Cadbury muses about what to call this two-volume work. He considers *Ad Theophilum I* and *Ad Theophilum II*, and finally concludes: "Hyphenated compounds are not typographically beautiful or altogether congenial to the English language, but in order to emphasize the historic unity of the two volumes addressed to Theophilus the expression 'Luke-Acts' is perhaps justifiable."[73] His phrase overcame its typographical stigma and was more congenial to the English language than he perhaps thought! Subsequent generations of scholars have latched onto the phrase and invested it with a variety of meanings. If at the end of this study, the reader is hesitant to remove the hyphen from the phrase perhaps at least agreement might be reached on the benefit of a clearer understanding of what is meant by the phrase, "Luke-Acts" — a more nuanced gloss on a term that bears different meanings.

[73] Cadbury, *Making,* 11.

CHAPTER

2

The Generic Unity
of Luke and Acts

"Luke and Acts *must* be treated as affiliated with one genre,"
asserts David Aune in his valuable survey of the genre of Luke
and Acts.[1] His view is a logical outcome of the reversal of the
traditional and canonical separation of Luke and Acts instigated
by the works of H. J. Cadbury.[2] The object of this chapter is to
raise questions about Aune's far from eccentric assertion and
thereby to contribute to the ongoing refinement of the questions concerning the unity of Luke and Acts.

Neither Aune nor, to our knowledge, anyone else has sought
to demonstrate this presumed necessity. This thesis derives from
the view that Luke and Acts are a single work in two volumes
and thus must represent a single genre. Inherent probability
does, of course, support the view that two books with related
prefaces, a common dedication, sequential subject matter, and
some common characters, not to mention common themes, will
be of the same form. But probability does not establish necessity.

The post-redaction-critical shift from emphasis on the manip-
ulation of sources to concentration on the text as a self-sufficient
literary product has established Luke and Acts as major controls
upon one another, rather than Luke as primarily a revision of

---

[1] Aune, *New Testament,* 80, pp. 17–157. See also our comments in chapter 1.

[2] For a recent survey of Cadbury's contributions to the study of Luke and
Acts, see Beverly Gaventa, "The Peril of Modernizing Henry Joel Cadbury";
Donald Jones, "The Legacy of Henry Joel Cadbury"; and Richard Pervo, "On
Perilous Things."

Mark and Acts as a document to be viewed (for better or worse) in the light of the Pauline corpus. Literary unity appears to require generic unity and gives rise to Aune's demand.

Recognition of one type of unity, for example, narrative unity, does not depend upon generic unity. R. Tannehill's exemplary two-volume study of the narrative unity of Luke and Acts does not address the question of genre. Few now engaged in the study of "Luke-Acts" deal in any depth with the question of form and some are content to address these (and other) works as more or less *sui generis* (formally unique).[3] The discovery of the narrative or other unity of Luke and Acts gives impetus to the presumption of generic unity but does not settle the question.

EVIDENCE OF THE EARLY CHURCH

The different early uses of and attestations for Luke and Acts do not lend support to the view that the work was a generic whole ruthlessly separated by canonizing hacks.[4] Justin's position is unclear, but he may have known both books.[5] Marcion explicitly rejected Acts (if Tertullian is to be trusted).[6] This decision appears to indicate that the works could be viewed as distinct prior to the inclusion of Luke in a Gospel collection.[7] Irenaeus, who sought, on the other hand, to establish the closest possible connection between the two books, did recognize them as separate works by a single author.[8] The first he registered among the Four

---

[3] Tannehill, for example, does not concern himself with the question of the form of Luke and Acts.

[4] For the reception of Acts in the early church, see the various critical commentaries, e.g., E. Haenchen *Acts*, 6–14. It is quite unlikely that Luke and Acts were ever issued for a "public" market outside of Christian communities.

[5] Haenchen (*Acts*, 8–9) believes that Justin knew Acts. This is still disputable.

[6] Tertullian implies that Marcion rejected Acts, *Adv. Marc.* 5.2,7; *Praescr.* 22.

[7] Aune (*New Testament*, 116) believes that the fourfold Gospel arose ca. 125 c.e. and that this collection caused the separation of Luke from Acts. This dating is too early. Irenaeus, for whom the plurality of the Gospels was a difficulty, had to argue vigorously for the collection of four. See Gamble, "Canon," 208–212.

[8] Irenaeus is thus the first known proponent of the view that Luke and Acts are the hermeneutical key to Paul.

Gospels; the second is designated in translation as *Doctrina Apostolorum* (Teaching of the Apostles).[9]

Clement distinguishes the second book by the title it still bears: Πράξεις τῶν Ἀποστόλων, which is arguably a generic designation.[10] The so-called "Muratorian Canon," if it is early,[11] also takes notice of distinct works and discusses them in different places.[12] The place of Acts in ancient lists and manuscripts varies.[13] One may safely conclude that the argument for generic unity draws little aid or comfort from the earliest witnesses. This lack may be of relatively minor concern to those engaged in purely literary analyses but should not be overlooked in the discussion of ancient literary models for Luke and Acts.

[9] Irenaeus, *A.H.* 3.14,4. This title indicates (not surprisingly) that Irenaeus wished the work to be understood as instruction.

[10] Clement, *Strom.* 5.12. On πράξεις, see Aune, *New Testament,* 78; Pervo, *Profit,* 179 n.140 with their references. This title is neither original nor a clearly generic designation. It does indicate that some, at least, in the second century understood the work as a record of noteworthy deeds.

[11] A. Sundberg ("Canon Muratori") proposes an Eastern provenance and fourth-century date for this work. H. Gamble ("Canon," 212–214) holds to the traditional date but admits that Sundberg has raised important questions.

[12] Lines 2–8 are devoted to Luke; 34–39 to Acts.

[13] The order of the "Cheltenham Canon" (ca. 360) is Matthew, Mark, John, Luke, thirteen Epistles of Paul, Acts, Revelation (see further comments on this list in chapter 1). The Council *in Trullo* (692) lists "The Acts of our Apostles" last, following, *1* and *2 Clement* and the eight books of the *Apostolic Constitutions.* Epiphanius (*Panarion,* 76) places Acts after the Pauline corpus. Codex Claromontanus (seventh century) lists Acts after Revelation and before *Hermas, Acts of Paul,* and the *Apocalypse of Peter.* Augustine (*De Doctr. Christ.,* 2.12) concludes with Jude, James, Acts, and Revelation. Jerome (*Epistle,* 53.8) takes note of Acts after the Pauline corpus, and adds his famous comment that it seems to narrate "unadorned history" (*nuda historia*) but would receive more attention if people would take note of the famous author. Pope Innocent I (*Ad Exsuperium Ep. Tolosanum*) likewise lists Acts just before Revelation, as do Isidore (*De Ordine Lib.*), and others as late as the twelfth century.

K. and B. Aland (*Text,* 49–50) regard it as generally understood that Acts first circulated as an independent book. After an early association with the Gospels (p⁴⁶, the first mss. to include Acts with the Gospels, and Bezae), the work was associated with the Catholic letters from the fourth century as part of what was called the *Apostolos.* For a convenient list of the contents of mss. including Acts, see Bruce, *Acts,* 77–79.

THE PURPOSE OF GENERIC ANALYSIS

The study of literary types is a comparative discipline based upon the presupposition that language has social and cultural contexts relevant to its meaning and that formal units of discourse cannot properly be understood without consideration of their social functions. A major objective of form criticism is the discovery of how typical audiences may have received particular works.[14]

For two generations the application of form criticism to the New Testament restricted itself mainly to oral and "non-literary" texts. A footnote to Overbeck and/or K. L. Schmidt once sufficed to dismiss "literature" proper from the New Testament scene, freeing scholars to pursue its literary and theological uniquenesses. The welcome demise of this procedure has left the discipline in a somewhat confused state.[15] So eagerly has research returned to the study of ancient literature and genres that the danger now exists of overlooking the obvious contrasts between early Christian texts in general and the sophisticated writings produced by and for those with the resources to receive and enjoy higher education. One cannot, for example, simply equate Pauline letters with specimens of learned epistolary rhetoric or the Gospels with biographies like those of Plutarch, however valuable such texts may be for lending profile to the subject. There are great differences in subject matter, style, and cultural level between such works and the New Testament, and therefore differences in expectations from audiences.[16] In general one may safely state that the authors of the New Testament writings lacked

---

[14] From the perspective of the "Sociology of Literature" this is the question of *Sitz im Leben.* In literary-critical terms the goal is to refine the profile of the authorial audience.

[15] Several volumes of the Westminster *Library of Early Christianity,* to cite but one example, attest to the shift away from distinguishing the NT from contemporary literature. For a comprehensive review of research, see K. Berger, "Hellenistische Gattungen."

[16] See Pervo (*Profit,* 5–8) for more detailed comments on these matters.

both the educational refinement to produce "elevated" discourse and hearers equipped with the education and interest to enjoy them.[17] Those who compare New Testament texts with the Greco-Roman literature of the classical curriculum must nearly always work with analogies, some of which are remote.

Freedom from cultured norms reaped a bonus in the creativity and flexibility available to those not bound by learned conventions. Many types of poetry and prose had their roots in "folk culture."[18] The old saw about the Gospels and Acts as *"sui generis"* (generically unique) has in its favor the recognition of the creative potential inherent within popular culture. So long as our repertory of truly "popular" ancient literature remains quite circumscribed, we shall be obliged to recognize that the comparison of New Testament texts to the writings of Josephus, Lucian, and Dio of Prusa, for example, will have limited results. No classification of Luke and Acts in ancient literary terms will enable these books to be shelved next to Thucydides, nor can such classifications fully illumine such issues as purpose or "accuracy."[19]

The application of a thoroughly rigorous theory of genre to Luke and Acts, such as the requirement that both volumes adhere to the same generic conventions, would be unwise. Lukas was, to a degree, venturing into *terra incognita*. The readers were unlikely to have been so particular about niceties, and it is not outrageous to suspect that this was an author who regarded

[17] The author of Hebrews approaches a high level of refinement but fails to qualify as either a philosopher or as a pure Greek stylist. Lukas strains to compose a few classical periods, not always with success (witness Acts 1:1-5 and 24:5-8). Pervo (*Profit,* 5–11) and M. A. Tolbert (*Sowing,* index *s.v.* "Popular Literature," 335) express reservations about the application of classical canons to the Gospels and Acts.

[18] Greek examples include epic, lyric, and dramatic poetry. Note also the contributions of popular storytelling to the development of Jewish and Greek historiography.

[19] One may observe that most efforts to place Luke and Acts within the context of ancient historiography have included a substantial amount of exculpation, with emphasis upon licenses available to ancient, but not to modern, historians. Resolution of the issue of genre will not in and of itself resolve the question of the author's intentions and efforts to present "truth."

models as bridges that might be burned once their purposes had been fulfilled.

The quest for a wide range of potentially comparable works reveals a gap between Luke and Acts. For the first volume there is a wealth of biographical material of varying type and quality, not to mention the other canonical Gospels. In the case of Acts, however, the basis for comparison is rather slim, particularly if the Apocryphal Acts are taken off the board before play properly begins.[20] The question of the genre or genres of Luke and Acts is acute because Acts is difficult to classify, not because of a dearth of analogies to Luke.

Traditional form criticism has tended to distinguish between Luke and Acts, having found for Luke a reasonably safe haven within the Gospel genre, while forced to let Acts drift amidst the capricious shoals of historiography, with shipwreck in store for many who press too quickly toward a secure haven.[21] As stated above, it is the emergent dominance of the unified Luke-Acts that has brought to the fore the question of a necessary common genre. In this endeavor Acts must take priority, and most of the proposals thus focus upon some facet of historiography.

MODERN PROPOSALS OF GENERIC UNITY

Cadbury dealt only briefly with the question of genre. After musing upon the merits of comparison with biography, history, and other genres, he concluded that Luke-Acts was more like history than anything else.[22] This tentative suggestion, so typical of Cadbury in its reserve, reveals the tension expressed by "biography" and "history," with their obvious applications.

[20] The Apocryphal Acts are not a homogenous collection revealing adherence to stringent generic principles.

[21] See Pervo, *Profit,* esp., 11–15. Implicit within the stated division is the problematic view that the first volume is a species of folk-literature and the second an example of learned prose.

[22] *Making,* 132–134. Cadbury did not view Luke and Acts as representatives of a single genre but rather saw genre as the reason for the separation of the two books (*ibid.,* 10, 134). See also Pervo, "On Perilous Things."

The Monograph

E. Plümacher and H. Steichele have built upon H. Conzelmann's modern proposal that the then popular monograph provides good parallels.[23] Conzelmann and his students have applied this notion primarily to the explication of Acts, although not in defense of the work's historical accuracy.[24] The merits of this approach are also its weaknesses, for the category was quite adaptable and diverse.

The monographic genre was congenial to exponents of the more sensational types of historiography, who wished to provide the cultured public with edifying light reading.[25] Insofar as they focused upon the public life of a famous figure, monographs could resemble biographies. As an aid to plot construction authors could exploit the resources of tragedy. Chariton's *Callirhoe*, the first fully extant romantic novel, was characterized as a monograph by Reitzenstein.[26] *3 Maccabees* is another candidate.[27] The monograph thus described is quite flexible, including romances, historical novels, semi-biographies, and specimens of history.[28] The description of Luke and Acts as

[23] W. Ramsay (*St. Paul*, 23) may have been the first to suggest this affiliation. He had Tacitus' *Agricola* in mind.

[24] Conzelmann offers some brief remarks in *Acts*, xl–xlii. See also Plümacher, *Lukas*, "Historiker," 262–263, "Monographie," "Acta-Forschung," 150–153; Steichele, "Vergleich der Apostelgeschichte." Cf. also K. Berger, "Gattungen," 1275, 1281; E. Richard, "Luke," 11. Plümacher ("Apostelgeschichte," 509–515) relates Acts to the tradition of "dramatic" or "tragic-pathetic" historiography in its mode. He views Luke and Acts as "two monographs loosely connected with one another" (515).

[25] The best known description of the function of the monograph refers to one that was never written: Cicero's invitation to Lucceius to make his consulship the subject of a piece, *Ad Fam.*, 5.12. The subject of such monographs, as the Latin exemplars confirm, was political and military history.

[26] *Hellenistische Wunderzählungen*, 94–99.

[27] Conzelmann, *Acts*, xl.

[28] B. MacQueen (*Myth*) opens his preface to a monograph on *Daphnis and Chloe* with a discussion of Sallust:

Anyone who must rely on Sallust as a source for Catiline's conspiracy, or the war against Jugurtha, can testify that Sallust is sometimes careless with (historical?) monographs is quite insightful, but it does not provide a great deal of specificity.[29] Works of several generic types could avail themselves of monographic structure and design. Monographs are, moreover, complete by definition. Luke and Acts cannot, because of their diversity and breadth, be viewed as a single monograph. To regard them as two (linked) monographs is a covert argument for some kind of disunity.

General History

Plümacher observes a tendency toward monographic collections in "Universal Histories."[30] This avenue has been fruitfully developed by D. Aune and, along related lines, by D. Balch.[31] History has not been kind to the general historians of antiquity.[32] Ephorus, the founder of this type, has not been well received by modern critics. Most universal historians survive only

---

his facts. Not only is he occasionally confused about chronology and geography, but he also invents incidents and puts sometimes unwarranted constructions on the motives of his characters. In short, he is anything but scrupulously objective; and on such grounds as these, he has more than once been accused of crossing that (putatively) sharp line that ought to separate history from fiction (p. ix).

MacQueen then takes note of various theories: Sallust lied, was tendentious, or knew nothing about writing history (p. x). One could be reading a "liberal" history of research on Luke and Acts! In MacQueen's view the problem is that Sallust has been condemned for doing other than he intended. The solution is to recognize that, "from a narratological perspective, then, Sallust has more in common with a novelist ... than with the modern historian" (p. xi).

[29] For additional references on this subject, see Pervo, *Profit*, 6–7. Plümacher's classification is cautiously hedged. He thinks that it is scarcely possible to locate Luke and Acts within one of the known Greco-Roman genres ("Historiker," 263). Monography was not by nature moralizing. Sallust may have had moral ends in view, but these are implicit, and, if he were a partisan, it is not easy to discover his position.

[30] He points to Diod. Sic., 16.1, "Historiker," 263. See also Fornara, *Nature of History*, 43.

[31] They prefer this translation to the more common "Universal History." See Aune, *New Testament*, 88–89; Balch, "Acts"; idem, "Comments."

[32] For a brief review of this type, see Fornara, *Nature of History*, 42–46.

in fragments.[33] Scarcely half of the best-preserved specimen, Diodorus Siculus, remains. Comparison is thereby rendered difficult, but by no means impossible.

General historians apparently wrote from some kind of understanding of world unity, whether political, as with Polybius,[34] or philosophical, as in the case of Posidonius.[35] Religious and other types of syncretism were grist for their mills. Since Lukas shares this view of human unity (see below, chapter 4), authors like Diodorus can, at the very least, provide useful background. What survives from the beginning of the Common Era, however, suggests a macro-genre, capable of subsuming within itself a variety of genres of diverse origin. Even if Luke and Acts were to be assigned to this comprehensive category, it would be appropriate to seek generic peculiarities in each volume.

The major problem with this categorization is the particularity of Luke and Acts[36] and Lukas's consequent need to make a case for this small Palestinian movement's claim to be a world religion.[37] The relatively limited scope of these books constitutes a barrier to regarding them as general history, for even the most nationalistic of general historians labored upon a much vaster canvass than that of Lukas. Luke and Acts represent the kind of sources utilized by general historians like Alexander Polyhistor.[38] For such historians local and national myth, legend,

---

[33] In the first century B.C.E. universal histories emerged in quantity, probably in response to the formation of the Roman Empire. Timagenes, Pompeius Trogus, Diodorus Siculus, Posidonius, and Nicolaus of Damascus all belonged to this era.

[34] On Polybius, see Adkins, *From the Many*, 173–176.

[35] These histories are general in their spatial view, but not in the temporal. Polybius, for example, wrote a continuation of Timaeus, Posidonius of Polybius.

[36] Aune is sensitive to this issue and presses for the importance of Luke's "National Consciousness," *New Testament*, 140–141.

[37] This is expressly formulated in the famous claim "not in a corner," Acts 26:26. Celsus (Origen, *Contra Celsum*, 4.36, 6.78) sneered at Jesus' origins "in a corner of Palestine." Luke 2:1-7 attempts to refute such criticism by relating the birth of Jesus in the context of a "universal census." On the general subject see Malherbe, *Paul and the Popular Philosophers*, 147–163.

[38] Polyhistor, via Eusebius, is the channel for the fragments of those "Hellenistic Jewish Historians" who provide stimulating parallels to Luke and Acts. For a modern edition and translation of these fragments, see Holliday, *Fragments*.

and history were the building blocks from which their comprehensive structures were formed.[39] No doubt many of these local authorities would have judged the incorporation of their writings into larger works with much different objectives to be nothing less than treason, as their own intention was to relate the particular to the general rather than to subsume the particular within it.

Antiquities

Balch, who assumes generic unity, focuses upon the type of historiography called "Antiquities," represented by Dionysius of Halicarnassus and his imitator, Flavius Josephus. He prefaces his comments with this same observation: "Neither one ethnic origin — Hebrew or Greek — nor one genre — biography, romance, historical monograph, or general history — will clarify the content and structure of these two books, which are a mixture on both counts."[40] His object is to point out various themes of Luke and Acts and thereby provide illumination for the cultural and ideological context of the work.

Comparisons between Lukas and Josephus are not wanting, thus Balch's focus upon Dionysius is most pertinent and welcome. The "Antiquities" format serves (ostensibly) to explain one group to another through description of its growth and development. The relevance of this outlook to Luke and Acts is clear.[41] There are also limitations. The two extant examples of this type are

---

Discussions of their relevance for Acts include Pervo, *Profit*, index *s.v.* "Artapanus," 209; Plümacher, "Historiker," 240; and Sterling, "Historiography."

[39] For one rationale of this procedure, see the Preface to Diod. Sic. 4.

[40] "Comments," 343.

[41] To cite but one example, Lukas stresses the antiquity of Christianity not only by placing it in continuity with Judaism but through use of ἀρχαῖος, (ancient) to denote the time of Christian origins (Acts 15:7, 21 [twice in a crucial chapter]; and 21:16. Cf. Luke 9:8). Note also ἀρχή (beginning; Luke 1:2); and, possibly, ἤρξατο (begin; Acts 1:1).

substantial works with ethnic, national, and military-political orientations.[42]

None of these subjects was of great use to Lukas, whose theme did not embrace the conventional topics of Greco-Roman historiography and who wished to demonstrate that Christianity was neither ethnic nor nationalistic. When Balch proposes that Lukas has substituted miraculous deeds for military exploits,[43] he reveals more contrast than comparison, for this shift is compatible with the concept of πράξεις (acts), which dealt with various personal achievements, and the orientation toward newer (nonepic) kinds of heroes, who spoke to groups less interested in traditional historiography. One offshoot from this road is the path that led toward romance.[44]

Aune and Balch point to pliable, fluid, and disparate types of historical writing, types that have contributions to make to the development of profiles for Luke and Acts but are probably too comprehensive and too different in theme and orientation to provide the primary model.[45] Comparison with Diodorus and Dionysius reveals that Lukas was familiar with contemporary techniques for explaining the origin and growth of an important phenomenon and could utilize them selectively for portraying

[42] The *Antiquities* of Josephus and Dionysius contain twenty books each, although the latter does not survive in full.

[43] "Comments," 353. The preceding pages (351–352) prepare the ground by noting Dionysius' reluctance to stress miracles. This is, however, a common trait of historians, who often supplied both "natural" and "miraculous" explanations for phenomena or events. The narrator of Luke and Acts identifies the two, places no distance between the reader and miraculous events, and offers no alternative etiologies. Most learned historians of the first century would regard this as a defect.

[44] This term tends to embrace a disparate mass of writings, including romantic novels, Apocryphal Acts, and hagiography, as well as the *Alexander-Romance* and kindred works.

[45] An important objection to this evaluation is that the narrator's subject was limited to two or three generations and that he thus had to adapt the model. If there were three volumes, the first covering "Biblical History," the case would be compelling. Rather than follow this line, however, Lukas does no more than summarize much of that history in speeches (Acts 7:2-53, 13:16-22).

Christianity as a worldwide movement.[46] This comparison also indicates that, when considered as a historian, Lukas was an amateur with some rhetorical training[47] and his work deals with (by formal standards) a questionable, if not contemptible, subject directed to an unworthy readership.[48]

Apologetic History

G. E. Sterling takes a focused look at some related material — the tradition of "Apologetic Historiography"[49] — which he traces

---

[46] Comparison of Luke and Acts with ancient historiography will, of course, take into account the variance between Lukas's picture of Christianity's standing and the reality of the situation.

[47] The narrator was capable of producing a fairly good style at particular points, such as Acts 15:23-30; 17:16-34; and 19:23-40, but limits are apparent. Acts 24:5-8, for example, strives to be a sentence but lacks a principal verb. Even these "showcase" pieces fall below the standards for learned historiography. Lukas's imitation of the LXX is indicative. On the one hand, as Plümacher (*Lukas*) has demonstrated in convincing detail, this practice is parallel to the Greco-Roman fondness for imitation. On the other hand, the model suggests that the authorial audience evidently found Septuagintal Greek quite acceptable. Josephus, to the contrary, improves upon rather than imitates the language of the LXX. R. L. Fox, (*Pagans and Christians,* 305) is quite blunt:

> His [Paul's] companion, the author of Acts, has also been mistaken for a Hellenistic historian and a man of considerable literary culture; in fact, he has no great acquaintance with literary style, and when he tries to give a speech to a trained pagan orator, he falls away into clumsiness after a few good phrases. His literary gifts lay, rather, with the Greek translation of Scripture, the Septuagint, which he knew in depth and exploited freely; to pagans its style was impossibly barbarous.

[48] The chief social function of Greco-Roman historiography was to contribute to the formation of (aristocratic) military and political leaders. The assumption that Luke and Acts belong within this literary orbit carries with it a potential challenge to the equally prevalent assumption that Lukas wrote for Christians in general. The prominence of leadership themes in both books would support the view that Christian leaders formed a substantial component of the implied readership. The notion that works like the Gospels were intended for direct consumption by large audiences engaged in private reading is anachronistic.

[49] "Luke-Acts and Apologetic Historiography," 326–342. See also his recent *Historiography and Self-Definition.*

from Greek ethnography, through Hellenistic efforts by "barbarian" authors to present in Greek dress the glorious antiquity of their native cultures, and, ultimately, into apologetic proper.[50] If the ostensible audience for such works was curious and open-minded Hellenes, native readers would find in them a basis for establishing their identity in a new world. They are often indirectly apologetic.

As are Luke and Acts. Sterling points to more than apologetic elements, however, for Lukas also strives to carve out an understanding of Christian identity in a world that is new for believers of both gentile and Jewish backgrounds. Antiquity, continuity, and group consciousness are qualities that contribute to this formation. Aune and Balch observe similar themes in the larger histories. Josephus overlaps both.[51] Most of the texts surveyed by Sterling are of relatively modest size, and some of them are of decidedly popular character. Through the introduction of smaller and more popular works, Sterling brings the discussion more closely into the cultural milieu of Luke and Acts. He has also opened the door to (biographical) romance.[52]

The proposals of Aune, Balch, and Sterling would be strengthened if Lukas were an early advocate of the view that Christians constitute a "Third Race" (in addition to Jews and Gentiles), even in the form of the Church as the "New Israel," for this would provide a nationalistic underpinning to the work and link it

---

[50] Sterling refers to the (fragmentary) works of Berossos, Manetho, and various Hellenistic Jewish historians.

[51] With his apology, *Against Apion,* and the *Jewish Antiquities,* a work in the pattern of Dionysius, Josephus provides examples of both of these types. The two works reflect different methods, and sometimes contradictory viewpoints.

[52] See the discussion of these and kindred writings in Pervo, *Profit,* 114–119; and "The Testament of Joseph and Greek Romance," in *Studies on the Testament of Joseph,* 15–28, ed. Nickelsburg. Among the more popular texts within this sphere are various "National Romances," which celebrated the exploits of such figures as Nectanebus and Sesonchosis. The *Alexander-Romance* exhibits some of these qualities. Artapanus, which is perhaps the most similar in style and structure to Luke and Acts among the works discussed by Sterling, is usually classified as a historical novel.

to the later Christian Apologists. Lukas, however, is not an exponent of this understanding of the Church, which is rather viewed as the "True Israel," including both Jews and Gentiles.

Biblical Historiography

At least since the time of C. C. Torrey and H. J. Cadbury there have been proposals to view Luke and Acts as continuations of the tradition of biblical history, in particular of the work of the Deuteronomist.[53] In the past decades this view has been variously presented by J. Drury, M. Hengel, D. Tiede, T. L. Brodie, D. Schmidt, W. Kurz, and D. Moessner.[54] Some scholars point to style, others to structure and organization. Nearly all have found theological congruence. Tiede and Moessner expound Lukan thought as a reflection of the Deuteronomic theology of history and seek to show how the Deuteronomic view of prophets has helped to shape Lukan Christology. Moessner regards Deuteronomy as the primary literary model for the central section of Luke.[55]

In the view of J. Drury, Lukas imitated Old Testament books on a large scale, using, for example, 1 Kings 8 as the model for Luke 1 and presenting John the Baptist as a new Samuel.[56] For Drury design has prominence over tradition. Lukas was in complete control of varied sources. To understand the Gospel

---

[53] C. C. Torrey, *The Composition and Date of Acts*; and H. J. Cadbury, *The Making of Luke-Acts,* xxx. Cadbury's vigorous opposition to Torrey's view that much of Luke and Acts was written in Aramaic has probably contributed to the neglect of Torrey's suggestions about the similarities between the works of Lukas and the Chronicler.

[54] J. Drury, *Tradition and Design;* M. Hengel, *Acts and the History of Earliest Christianity;* D. Tiede, *Prophecy and History in Luke-Acts;* T. L. Brodie, "Greco-Roman Imitation"; D. Schmidt, "The Historiography of Acts"; W. Kurz, "Narrative Models"; and D. Moessner, *Lord of the Banquet; idem,* "Bios."

[55] The "Travel Narrative," Luke 9:51–19:44, in Moessner's reckoning.

[56] *Tradition,* 3–8, 58–59.

one must look to the Old Testament rather than to Mark.[57] Moessner takes strong exception to redaction criticism.[58] In some rather brief, suggestive remarks M. Hengel does address the question of genre. Those seeking a model for Luke and Acts should look "in the accounts of history to be found in the Old Testament and Judaism, which to a large degree are composed of 'biographical' sections."[59] Hengel points to the stories of the patriarchs, followed by the life of Moses and then the history of the conquest under Joshua's leadership as a narrative sequence that would have been familiar.[60] He thus touches upon the question of succession, an issue that gave impetus to C. Talbert's proposals regarding the genre of Luke and Acts.[61]

Despite Cadbury's observations and occasional comments by others, there has been little detailed investigation of the significance of 1 and 2 Maccabees, particularly the latter, as models for Lukas.[62] This neglect may reflect some apologetic concerns. Heirs of the Protestant Reformation generally exclude 1 and 2 Maccabees from consideration as Scripture. If Luke and Acts can be understood in terms of Hebrew biblical roots alone they are free from contamination by "pagan" culture (and can more easily be assigned an early date).

Historical method offers no consolation to such views. The contrast between "Jewish" and "Hellenistic" rarely bestows a useful perspective.[63] When strictly applied to Luke and Acts it

---

[57] Drury regards Matthew as a principal Lukan source.

[58] *Lord,* 3–7.

[59] Hengel, *Acts,* 32.

[60] Still Hengel is finally willing to label Acts as a monograph (*Acts,* 36).

[61] See also Tiede, *Prophecy and History,* 17. On Talbert, see below, pp. 36–37.

[62] Those who regard Luke and Acts as monographs do not neglect these works. See Cadbury, *Making,* 115, 230 n. 28, 322; Conzelmann, *Acts,* xl; and Berger, "Gattungen," 1275, 1281. Kurz ("Narrative Models," 181) locates Luke-Acts somewhere between 1 and 2 Macc. As a characterization of Acts this is apposite. For Luke it presents some difficulties.

[63] Although the subtitle of Schmidt's article, "Deuteronomistic or Hellenistic," would seem to imply a firm separation between Judaism and Hellenism, his analysis is more sophisticated.

leaves such elements as the prefaces, the dedications, and, above all, the speeches in Acts out of the picture. These items are clear indicators that, insofar as Lukas is to be regarded as a historian and to be interpreted from the context of early Judaism, Jewish history written in Greek should form a major element of the context, as well as Greek historiography in general. Lukas read the Bible in Greek and through Greek eyes. Balch notes that Van Seters, who is an important authority for Schmidt, compares Deuteronomy with Herodotus.[64]

An equally undesirable approach is to insist upon the choice between Lukas as exponent of a Deuteronomic view of history or as representative of a Greek providential interpretation of history. The two are not incompatible. Both bring insights to the world of the author and the audience. The relations between such concepts are subtle; premature efforts to exclude one or the other will limit the discussion.

The advocates of biblical models behind Luke and Acts can make a rather better case for illuminating the narrator than the implied readers. Was the audience expected to perceive these two books as Deuteronomic? The question is relevant to this discussion because genre is an aspect of communication. At issue is how the authorial audience would have viewed these books rather than which models the author employed to provide shape and viewpoint to the text. The formal features of Greek historiography used by Lukas are strong evidence that the implied reader was to be familiar with these conventions.

Those who relate Luke and Acts to biblical history are more interested in the sources of ideas and patterns than in genre. There is, in fact, no such genre as "Biblical Historiography," but rather a number of genres with roots in the Ancient Orient and branches in the Hellenistic world. This is an important avenue for research but not the path that has yet laid open the way to the genre of Luke and Acts.

---

[64] "Acts as Hellenistic Historiography."

Philosophical Succession

Charles Talbert has made a more sustained case than most others for a common biographical genre, focusing on the histories of succession developed amidst philosophical school conflicts.[65] He engages a vital Lukan concern, the demonstration of legitimacy through continuity. The pattern Talbert wishes to elucidate derives from the collection of Diogenes Laertius and includes a life of the founder, data about successors, and fundamental doctrines. Aune has objected that this pattern is relatively rare in Diogenes[66] and that succession lists are not to be equated with narratives.

Christians from the second century onward did adopt a kindred model, beginning with Hegisippus. Luke and Acts do not reflect this procedure. Only by inference can one detect succession in these books, for the narrator does not explain the fate of the apostles, the emergence of πρεσβύτεροι (elders)[67] and ἐπίσκοποι (overseers, bishops),[68] the ascendence of James to leadership, or the links among these developments. Indeed, arguments for succession as later understood would have weakened Lukas's case for Paul, since the latter, as was well known, was neither a disciple of Jesus nor one of the "Twelve."[69] Lukas has, in essence, finessed the succession question by his portrait of Paul's relationship to the Jerusalem church and by his avoidance of the difficult relations between the Twelve and the relatives of Jesus. The philosophical succession model would have presented Lukas with major disadvantages.

[65] *Literary Patterns,* 125–140. See also, *What is a Gospel?* 91–127, and above, pp. 14–16.

[66] *New Testament,* 141.

[67] Lukas is sufficiently fond of this office to associate it with Paul (Acts 14:23).

[68] Lukas apparently did not approve of bishops. Emergent ideas of monoepiscopacy (cf. Ignatius) may account for this view.

[69] Irenaeus does establish somewhat delicate chains of succession (and inferences of the same) from the available resources. In this endeavor the image of Luke, companion of Paul and author of Luke and Acts, assumed great importance.

Talbert's argument takes serious account of the existence and content of the two books and seeks a new approach toward a long-standing problem. His fresh perspective has caused scholars to reconsider the entire question of the genre of Luke and Acts. This quest may be the most important result of his contribution. His specific theory, however, has not met with general approval.[70]

DIFFERENCES BETWEEN LUKE AND ACTS

Canonical separation has not been the single reason for regarding Luke and Acts as generically different. The constituent forms of Luke (for example, sayings, miracles, and parables) are shared with the other Synoptics, so that much of the Gospel yields to traditional form-critical analysis, but this is not the case with Acts. The contrasting approaches of Martin Dibelius to Luke and Acts illustrate this difference, just as they established the patterns for subsequent research.[71]

Claims that the differences between Luke and Acts are to be explained by reference to the sources used in each do not resolve the question. Lukas was quite capable of introducing into the Gospel episodic pieces and scenes like those so typical of Acts, scenes constructed from small units and (apparently) imagination.[72] Moreover, the type of sources selected or available is not without relevance to the issue of genre. Finally, the picture of Luke the Evangelist as a figure hog-tied by his sources scarcely represents the cutting edge of Lukan studies.

The foremost examples of the use of different material and methods are the famous speeches of Acts, compositions of the

[70] See M. Parsons, "Reading Talbert."

[71] Dibelius, *From Tradition to Gospel* (Luke); and *Studies,* 1–25 (Acts). For the impact of Dibelius upon subsequent research, see Haenchen, *Acts,* 34–41; and Bruce, *Acts,* xvi.

[72] Luke 4:16-30 is the best-known example of this technique. The various symposia (for example Luke 5:29-39; 7:36-50; 14:1-24; 22:14-38) are additional instances.

author that exhibit some knowledge of contemporary rhetorical models.[73] Did Lukas have the license of a historian to invent appropriate speeches only in Acts? The presence of these numerous addresses remains a formidable obstacle to the case for generic unity. They are one of the most prominent indicators that in Acts Lukas has other literary goals and thus possibly operated with a different set of generic conventions. The speeches of Acts mark the second book as different.

Both Luke and Acts utilize journeys as structural (and symbolic) devices. The content of these respective journeys reveals important contrasts. The gospel journey of Jesus to Jerusalem (Luke 9:51–19:44) is somewhat artificial.[74] There is relatively little information about the itinerary, resting places, etc. The narrator takes pains to state that Jesus and the disciples were engaged in a journey but shares little about it. Instead, the text is replete with teaching. The gospel journey is thus a medium for presenting Jesus as an itinerant preacher of the "Way." The travel reports of Acts, on the other hand, are often rich with circumstantial detail and prefer accounts of missionary experience to sermons on ethical topics. In Luke, Jesus serves as a model primarily in his passion. The leaders depicted in Acts exemplify their faith by deeds throughout the narrative. For this reason the book gained the title Πράξεις (Acts).[75]

Readers who proceed from Luke to Acts will note differences of tone. The Gospel offers many examples of forgiveness for sinners, whereas in Acts those who commit wicked deeds are liable to pay a stiff price. These punishments play an important role in both the plot and the implicit message of the book.

[73] See the comments and analysis by Krodel (*Acts*), Tannehill, (*Narrative Unity of Acts*), and the relevant articles of Kurz and Veltmann.

[74] Moessner (*Banquet*) offers a recent and comprehensive study of this material.

[75] These remarks do not imply that the two books are not complementary, nor do we wish to suggest that the experiences of the various missionaries in Acts are not imitations of Christ. The narratives of Acts are often evocative of the Passion (and Resurrection). These important literary and theological relationships remain independent of the question of generic unity.

Framing the text are Judas's gruesome death and Paul's miraculous survival of storm and poison (Acts 1:15-19; 27:1−28:10). Instead of Levi and Zacchaeus there is Ananias and Sapphira.[76] Curse, blinding, injury, ruin, hunger, and death await enemies of the Way.[77] Harlots and publicans are not among the featured members of the community as they are in Luke. Those who are named are likely to be persons of some status or wealth.[78] The urban poor are viewed with disdain.[79] Even Ephesian artisans and citizenry are portrayed as labile and fickle (Acts 19:23-40). One would be somewhat hard-pressed to illustrate the Sermon on the Plain (Luke 6:20-49) by reference to Acts.[80] The radical tone of the gospel exhortations is muted. There are also some important differences in characterization. The disciples, in particular Peter, change greatly in understanding, vision, and ability.[81] In Luke the Pharisees are willing to entertain and listen to Jesus on occasion, but receive harsh criticism for their

[76] Levi: Luke 5:27-32; Zacchaeus: Luke 19:1-10; Ananias and Sapphira: Acts 5:1-11.

[77] Curse: 8:20-21; blinding: 9:1-9; 13:11; injury: 19:13-17; ruin: 16:16-19; 19:23-40; hunger: 23:12-35; death: 1:16-18; 12:20-23. Zechariah's loss of speech is the only punitive miracle in Luke, and this is quickly reversed (1:20, 64).

[78] See Pervo, *Profit*, 77–81.

[79] Ibid., 34–38.

[80] The shift is not complete, but there is a difference. It is interesting to note that R. J. Cassidy deemed it necessary to follow up his work on the social ethics of Luke (*Political Issues*) with *Society and Politics in the Acts of the Apostles*. In this useful book Cassidy has had to shift his ground and focus on political questions regarding Paul. In Acts only Jewish authorities are fundamentally unworthy of trust, while wealth is acceptable if used in a proper manner.

[81] The explanation of this change by reference to the instructions of the risen Christ (Luke 24−Acts 1) and the gift of the Spirit (which does not explain Peter's role in Acts 1) does not obviate these changes. Lukas greatly modified the Markan portrait of Jesus' disciples (Brown, *Apostasy;* and most commentaries), suggesting that the characterization of them in Acts is closer to the Lukan ideal. For Chrysostom (*Homily 1,* 1) this change was an inducement to reading Acts:

> Here again you will see the Apostles themselves, speeding their way as on wings over land and sea; and those same men, once so timorous and void of understanding, on the sudden become quite other than they were; men despising wealth, and raised above glory and passion and concupiscence, and in short all such affections: moreover, what unanimity there is among them now!

attitudes and practices. In Acts, however, they are often supportive of the movement.[82]

These differences[83] indicate that Lukas approached Acts with
objectives and methods different from those which governed
the composition of Luke. At the very least they provide methodological justification for challenging the assumption of
generic unity.

POSSIBLE MODELS

What grounds might Lukas have had for presenting two con-
secutive volumes of differing literary types? In the first place,
we reiterate that Lukas required no justification of the sort
required by formal "rules," for he was producing a fundamentally
popular work and did not have to justify his composition in
the salons of the aristocracy or to the minds of the elite.[84] The
continuation of the gospel story was required by his theological
vision and by the need to vindicate the Pauline heritage.[85] These
requirements constituted for the author a priority far more
important than any need for literary justification.

[82] Nearly all of the passages adduced to show that the Pharisees are given
a more positive treatment in Luke and Acts than elsewhere are derived
from Acts.

[83] For theological differences, see chapter 4; for literary differences, see
chapter 3.

[84] This assertion is valid despite the apparent implications of the preface
and dedication to κράτιστος ("most excellent," a title otherwise used only in
addressing the Roman governors) Theophilus. Lukas may, to be sure, have
wished that this were the case and happily portrays his heroes in these settings,
but cultivated pagans would have found Luke and Acts offensive, inferior, and
frequently unintelligible.

[85] Conzelmann (*Theology of St. Luke*) set forth the first sustained argument
for and description of the importance of continuity in Lukan theology. His
many critics have almost without exception accepted this interpretation. Esler
(*Community*) approaches the theme of legitimation of the gentile mission from
a sociological perspective. At the core of all matters related to the unities of
Luke and Acts is the question of why Lukas composed a second book.

Secondly, we can point to one prototype most certainly available: the Greek Bible.[86] Within this disparate corpus Lukas would have encountered such collections as 1–4 Kingdoms, 1–2 Esdras,[87] and 1–2 (perhaps also 3–4) Maccabees. Each would have appeared as an individual volume within a group, although by our standards they represent a variety of literary types.[88] These precedents would have provided Lukas with any needed warrant for issuing two volumes of differing genres. In this, as in other respects, Lukas may well have followed patterns set by biblical historians.

ANCIENT COLLECTIONS

Rationales for the division of ancient works into discreet books and for the collection of writings into corpora varied greatly. In some cases division followed composition after a long interval. Homer is an example of this process. Vergil's epic, on the other hand, represents divisions that reflect the author's artistic plan. Still other collections grew over time with the addition of subsequent "books." The Bible is the best-known, but by no means the only, example of this process.[89] Technical factors, especially the need to limit rolls to manageable length, also applied.[90] The history of the Pauline corpus provides illustrations of differing division, arrangement, and contents. There are no firm rules for ancient book division to which one may appeal, particularly since the New Testament witnesses do not give evidence of the use of rolls.[91]

[86] See the discussion of Biblical Historiography above, pp. 33–35.

[87] The problems of the differences in content and enumeration of the various works of the Chronicler are not material to this discussion.

[88] The original titles of Luke and Acts (if any existed) are, of course, unknown.

[89] The development of the *Mishnah* and the *Talmud(s)* illustrate one such type of formation. Another is the dubious or spurious works that accrued to the collections of numerous ancient writers.

[90] A famous example of this is the division between books I and II of Josephus' *Contra Apionem*, discussed in chapter 3.

[91] The view that Luke and Acts first appeared in rolls is only a hypothesis,

In the case of Luke and Acts the situation is quite different. Despite some textual problems at the boundary between the two books and occasional suggestions that the opening of Acts is secondary, there is general agreement today that the division between Luke and Acts is neither arbitrary nor accidental, whatever the length of a roll.[92] The first volume is complete and self-contained. Acts is, in several senses, a new departure, but history has shown that it may be read, with at least modest profit and mild delight, independently of the Gospel, however less enriching such a reading may be. Closure and openness mark the conclusion of both books. Neither ancient practices regarding book division, technical limitations, nor observable literary intentions support the hypothesis that the disjunction between Luke and Acts is too insignificant to justify investigation of generic disunity.

CANONICAL ISSUES

Current emphasis upon the unity of Luke and Acts implicitly or explicitly regards the canonical separation of the two as an error to be remedied by criticism. The obvious cause of this error, if it is such, is the canonical proclivity for arranging material by (collected) genres rather than by presumed authors.[93] Acts occupies different places in manuscripts and canon lists, but is never directly linked to Luke. The received shape of the New Testament Canon[94] exhibits a sensitivity to differences of genre and type. The proposal that Acts became separated from Luke because of the four-gospel collection[95] begs the question,

---

not only because the autograph is lost, but also because all of the extant witnesses employ the codex.

[92] On the division between Luke and Acts, see Parsons, *Departure.*

[93] An example of generic arrangement is the Johannine Epistles and Revelation, which did not find a home in relation to the Fourth Gospel, despite views about their authorship.

[94] Gospels, Acts, Pauline letters (a) to churches; (b) to individuals, Hebrews, general letters, Revelation.

[95] See above, n. 7.

for genre was the grounds for that putative separation. The canonical arrangement provides a stronger argument for generic disparity than it does for the obfuscation of generic unity.

CONCLUSION

Since form criticism has value only if it makes a substantial contribution to understanding, those who stipulate a common genre for Luke and Acts are obliged to present more than a vague label that will facilitate examination of the reunited work, a procedure that requires no such justification. The unity of Luke and Acts is not a hypothesis requiring generic identity, and insistence upon such unity may well obscure the valuable insights to be gained from investigation of aretalogies, novels, apocryphal acts, various types of monographs, different modes of historical writing, biographies of diverse kinds, and other "gospels." Precisely because no analogy can fully suffice, particularly with regard to Acts, and most proposals have shed light upon the texts, the requirement for a single genre may impose unwelcome restrictions. The results of research suggest that much can be learned about Luke and Acts by studying them from *different* generic perspectives.

Then there is the text itself. Does it imply a work of one genre in two volumes? The preface to Acts states that the subject of the first book was the deeds and teachings of Jesus.[96] Acts 1:2-8 then focuses upon the apostles. This introductory material thus explains the traditional title of the second volume and justifies classification of the first as a biography.

Finally, if the argument for generic unity is pressed vigorously, Luke must be regarded as nothing more than half of a work rather than as a Gospel.[97] What then could be made of Matthew,

---

[96] The view that words and deeds must correspond was an ancient ethical commonplace and a primary basis for character evaluation in biographies.

[97] See above, pp. 13–16.

Matthew, Mark, and John? The argument for generic unity is liable to begin in obscurity and threatens to end in absurdity, the obscurity of eliminating many useful bases of comparison for the sake of a nebulous general model, and the absurdity of challenging the completeness of any Gospel.[98] If the unity of Luke and Acts is not a modern construct, the demand for generic unity very probably is.

[98] This remark refers to hypothetical extremes rather than to the thesis of any one author. Specifically, it is not intended to disparage or dismiss the proposals and findings of the scholars discussed in this chapter.

3

The Narrative Unity of Luke and Acts

Literary critics are usually more concerned with the unity of the story than with the unity of Luke's theology.[1] Several scholars have recently affirmed the assumption that Luke and Acts were intended to form one continuous, unified narrative from the perspective of the newer narrative criticism. Robert Tannehill, in his two-volume work, *The Narrative Unity of Luke-Acts*, claims: "The following study will emphasize the unity of Luke-Acts. This unity is the result of a single author working within a persistent theological perspective, but it is something more. It is a *narrative* unity, the unity appropriate to a well-formed narrative."[2] In the second volume, Tannehill nuances his position more carefully with regard to the issue of unity: "In spite of the title of my work, it is not a monograph arguing as a single, central thesis that Luke-Acts is a unified narrative. It presents much evidence of unity in Luke-Acts and shows how unity is maintained through narrative developments, but it neither argues that this unity is perfect nor focuses on this issue as its sole concern."[3]

From a similar perspective, Joseph Tyson has argued "the two books were intended to be read consecutively and that they tell a single story that begins with Zechariah in Jerusalem and ends with Paul in Rome."[4] Such statements illustrate the shift in

---

[1] A distinction made by Stephen Moore, "Narrative Commentaries," 29–62.
[2] Robert C. Tannehill, *Narrative Unity*, 1:xiii.
[3] Ibid., 2:8.
[4] Joseph B. Tyson, *The Death of Jesus in Luke-Acts*, ix–x.

American scholarship from Mark to Acts as the "primary" control for the interpretation of the Gospel of Luke.[5]

To decide whether or not Luke and Acts represent a narrative unity, the distinctions of the term "narrative" must be pressed. Seymour Chatman has distinguished between narrative as *discourse* and narrative as *story:* "In simple terms, the story is the *what* in a narrative that is depicted, discourse the *how*."[6] Chatman's work had a great impact on the early narrative analyses of biblical scholars and is still highly regarded in circles of biblical narratology.[7] Robert Funk's appropriation of Chatman's model is typical. For him, narrative as *discourse* refers "to the linguistic medium, to the words and sentences spoken or written in telling a story."[8] Narrative as *story*, on the other hand, refers "to what is told, to the actions and actors portrayed in the discourse, rather than to the words or statements of the expression. It is the subject of the story in contrast to the medium through which the subject is expressed."[9] This chapter examines the narrative unity of Luke and Acts at the level of discourse. The question of unity at the level of story will be pursued at the end of the chapter.

NARRATION IN LUKE AND ACTS

At the level of *discourse*, that is, the way the story is told, several objections may be registered against the premise that Luke and Acts form a narrative unity. That assertion has yet to be tested using the most recent developments in biblical narratology. By examining the narration of Luke and Acts from a literary-critical

[5] See Stephen D. Moore, "Narrative Commentaries," 32.

[6] Chatman, *Story and Discourse,* 19.

[7] See Culpepper, *Anatomy;* Rhoads and Michie, *Mark as Story;* Kingsbury, *Matthew as Story;* et al.

[8] Robert W. Funk, *Poetics,* 1.

[9] Ibid. In these definitions, Funk also distinguishes narrative as performance which is "the act of narrating, to the telling itself as an event" (p. 2).

perspective, some insight may be gained into the question of the narrative unity of those writings.

One of the principal means literary critics use to probe the discourse of a narrative is close attention to the narrator, the voice which speaks to the readers and tells the story.[10] In the apt words of Alan Culpepper, the narrator

> introduces us to the world of the narrative, explains what we must know to grasp it, and introduces the characters who populate the narrative world and the cultural codes which operate within it. The narrator relates the events which take place in the story, provides commentary which draws us to view the story as he or she understands it, and at points provides the reader with inside views of a character's thoughts or motives.[11]

Distinctions among the real author, the implied author, and the narrator are basic to the most elementary reading of literary theory. But that distinction seems to have been blurred even in the recent work of most narrative critics. Certainly it is understandable that gospel critics tend to collapse the categories of implied author and narrator, but of the New Testament narrative materials, only Luke and Acts presumably share a common real author. No one, however, has yet compared the narration, the discourse, of one with the other. The question is: can the same author produce two narratives which are distinct at the level of discourse? Or, in more carefully nuanced literary terms: can the same real author produce two distinct narrators or perhaps even two implied authors?[12]

The answer to this question is complex. A brief look at the history of Lukan scholarship may point in the right direction. Martin Dibelius asserted that "in Acts, Luke has employed a much

---

[10] On narration in the gospels, see Steven Sheeley, "The Narrator in the Gospel."

[11] R. Alan Culpepper, "Commentary on Biblical Narratives."

[12] Both narrator and implied author will be examined, the former in much more detail.

higher standard of writing than in the Gospel."[13] Likewise, C. K.
Barrett commented on the differences in style between the two:
"In the second volume, Luke is not merely a compiler of traditions, but an author."[14] These scholars were commenting from
the perspective of form and source analyses, but they do
demonstrate that differences between these two narratives have
long been noted. Even the fact that Robert Tannehill chose
different literary strategies for dealing with the two narratives
attests to the literary differences between the two volumes.[15] The
"literary swerve" in New Testament studies has provided the tools
necessary for a closer examination of those differences.

Scholars have successfully employed a number of models in
the study of New Testament narratives.[16] For the present task,
the model of Shlomith Rimmon-Kenan commends itself.[17] Her
taxonomy is simple, flexible and accessible, precisely the qualities
required of literary-critical models that are going to be applied
to biblical narratives.[18] Rimmon-Kenan's "typology of narrators"

[13] Martin Dibelius, *Studies in the Acts of the Apostles,* 2.

[14] C. K. Barrett, *Luke the Historian,* 27. Barrett may have drawn this insight
from Dibelius.

[15] In volume 1 Tannehill analyzes Luke by tracing the relationship of Jesus
with significant groups within the story, and in volume 2 he approaches Acts
in a sequential order from beginning to end. He claims (*Narrative Unity,* 2:5)
"that there are literary reasons why this is more advantageous in Acts than in
Luke," and states that those reasons emerge from the differences between the
two writings at the level of narration.

[16] Norman Petersen, "Point of View"; David Rhoads and Donald Michie, *Mark
as Story;* and Alan Culpepper, *Anatomy* all make use of the model developed
by Russian formalist, Boris Uspensky in *A Poetics of Composition.* Wayne Booth's
taxonomy of narration was employed by Robert Fowler (*Loaves and Fishes*) and
Charles Hedrick ("Narrator and Story"). In a dissertation on "The Narrator
of Acts," Allen Walworth pressed into service the work by Susan Lanser. Recently,
Jeffrey Staley (*The Print's First Kiss*) has made use of the models of Seymour
Chatman and Gérard Genette in his discussion of narration in John's Gospel.
For a summary of these works, see Steven Sheeley, "The Narrator in the Gospel."

[17] Shlomith Rimmon-Kenan, *Narrative Fiction.* Rimmon-Kenan uses the term
"narration" to describe narrative levels and voices, as well as speech represen-
tation (see chaps. 7 and 8 of her work).

[18] Literary-critical models developed for the study of modern literature are
not always suitable because they are designed for very complex narrative
structures.

describes narration in terms of narrative level, extent of participation in the story, and degree of perceptibility, and is well suited for a comparison of the narration of Luke and Acts.[19]

Narrative Level

According to Rimmon-Kenan, the "narrative level" to which the narrator belongs is a crucial factor "in the reader's understanding of and attitude to the story."[20] She draws a basic distinction between an *extradiegetic* narrator and an *intradiegetic* narrator. An extradiegetic narrator is one "who is, as it were, 'above' or superior to the story he narrates. . . ."[21] A narrator, on the other hand, is intradiegetic "if the narrator is also a diegetic character in the first narrative told by the extradiegetic narrator. . . ."[22]

Rimmon-Kenan further distinguishes between different levels of the narrative.[23] The narrator is telling the story on the first or primary level. A character in a story who tells another story is functioning on the second narrative level (i.e., a narrative within the first narrative). Robert Funk helpfully elaborates these differences with an analysis of the parable of the Prodigal Son:

---

[19] Ibid., pp. 94–103. As Steven Sheeley ("The Narrator in the Gospel," 14) has noted, "The value of Rimmon-Kenan's model lies both in its simplicity (other models are so complex in their formulation as to prohibit application) and in its comprehensive nature." Rimmon-Kenan also deals with the category of "reliability." The idea of an unreliable narrator seems to be a rather modern (in some cases postmodern) development in literary theory and since most biblical narrative critics agree that the Gospels (as well as all other literature of antiquity) show little or no evidence of literary unreliability, this analysis will not address that category. See, however, the studies of Charles Hedrick and Stephen Moore's lengthy discussion of James Dawsey's book in which Moore claims that for Dawsey the narrator of Luke is unreliable although Dawsey never uses the term per se.

[20] Ibid., 94.

[21] Ibid.

[22] Ibid. Rimmon-Kenan borrows these terms and those which follow under "Extent of Participation in the Story," from Genette.

[23] See Funk, *Poetics*, 31–33. Funk prefers the term hyperdiegetic for Rimmon-Kenan's extradiegetic.

Narrator	Narrative Level	Narratee
hyperdiegetic: Luke	first narrative: Gospel of Luke	hyperdiegetic: Theophilus
intradiegetic: Jesus	second narrative: Parable of the Prodigal	intradiegetic: tax collectors, etc.
hypodiegetic: servant	third narrative: recap of events	hypodiegetic: older son

Luke is the hyperdiegetic [or extradiegetic] narrator of the Gospel of Luke. Jesus is an intradiegetic narrator; the stories he tells belong to the second narrative. In the second part of the parable of the Prodigal Son, the servant meets the older son coming in from the field and tells him what has happened. His recounting of the reception of the younger son by the father (Luke 15:27) amounts to a story within a story, which is also within the Gospel of Luke, another story. That makes the servant's recapitulation a third narrative.[24]

On the first narrative level of both Luke and Acts the narrator functions primarily as an extradiegetic narrator, that is, he is "superior" to or removed from the story he tells. One point does, however, begin to distinguish the narrative voice of Luke from that of Acts. The narrator of Acts, of course, does intrude into the narrative in the so-called "we" passages, making the narrator an intradiegetic narrator for an extended portion of the Acts account. This technique will be treated below, pp. 65–67.

At the second level of narration, both narratives employ characters as intradiegetic narrators. Luke employs Jesus as an intradiegetic narrator who tells stories or parables. Especially important in this are the longer narrative parables like the Good

[24] Funk, *Poetics,* 32.

Samaritan (10:30-35), the Great Banquet (14:16-24), the Prodigal
Son (15:11-32), the Rich Man and Lazarus (16:19-31), the Ten
Pounds (19:11-27), and the Tenants (20:9-16), among others.
Likewise, Acts uses characters as narrators within the story (Peter,
Paul); thus Luke and Acts employ similar strategies in terms of
the first and second narrative levels.

On this second level of narration, however, the function of
Jesus' voice is distinguishable from the voice of the narrator.[25]
Jesus speaks in parables; the narrator never does. In Acts, the
voices of the narrator and the protagonists are more difficult
to differentiate. Within the speeches of Acts are language, style,
and content remarkably similar to that used by the narrator of
Acts. Furthermore, the voice of Jesus in Luke is clearly distinct
from that of his followers in Acts. That the narrator of Acts did
not depict the followers of Jesus as speaking in parables is not
unusual, since parables were a part of Jesus' characteristic peda-
gogical strategy. Still, the fact that the parables have been embedded in narrative texts is witness to the fact that disciples
obviously *did* tell parables; at least they repeated Jesus' parables
or attributed them to him. It is therefore not very farfetched
to question why in the narrative of Acts the disciples, who do
repeat Jesus' miraculous deeds, do not imitate his words. John,
on the other hand, shows that a narrative gospel may contain
long speeches but lack parables. In other words, Luke and Acts
would share much more in common at the discourse level if
either the speech of the protagonists in Acts (especially the Lukan
Peter who had heard Jesus' teachings) had imitated that of the
protagonist (Jesus) in Luke, or vice versa.

Rimmon-Kenan's categories cannot be dismissed as applicable
only to complex modern narratives. Gérard Genette noted:
"Second-degree narrative is a form that goes back to the very
origins of epic narrating, since Books IX-XII of the *Odyssey*, as

---

[25] See James Dawsey, *The Lukan Voice*, "Appendix C." Dawsey's conclusion that
there is dissonance between the viewpoints of the narrator and Jesus is
debatable.

we know, are devoted to the narrative Ulysses makes to the assembled Phaeacians."[26] Such second-degree narration, then, is at least as old as Homer, and the distinction between Luke's narrator who employs it regularly, and the narrator of Acts who does not, is a crucial one.

First-Level Narration

The distinctions, however, are pervasive. Even when both narrators function as extradiegetic, they employ various literary devices.[27] Older critical works addressed this issue under the auspices of stylistic and philological studies of New Testament writings — the stock and trade of professional biblical scholars for well over a century.[28] Statistical studies in terms of word frequency and usage have been an important piece of evidence in many of the disputes surrounding the authorship questions of many of the Epistles. Of course, such stylistic studies have been employed to debate the identity of the author of Luke and Acts (e.g., the Harnack/Hobart vs. Cadbury debate) as well as the relationship between the two writings (as in the proposal of A. C. Clark and its subsequent refutations by Knox and Argyle).

James Dawsey raised similar questions in a recent article.[29] After a detailed examination of some of the grammar and word usage in Luke and Acts, he concludes:

On the one hand, there is great similarity between the styles of Acts and Luke. On the other hand, there are some differences that need

---

[26] Genette, *Narrative Discourse,* 231.

[27] Rimmon-Kenan discusses this aspect of narration in a separate chapter. Since literary techniques are the effort of the narrator, it seems best to discuss such literary conventions here.

[28] Philological analysis began in the patristic period, a notable example of which is Origen, whose comments remain valuable.

[29] James Dawsey, "The Literary Unity of Luke-Acts," 65.

to be explained before too easily assuming that the two writings are actually one narrative.

Many of the differences Dawsey observes had already been noted by Albert Clark and before him by John Hawkins.[30] Hawkins's comment, now over eighty years old, about the linguistic similarity between Luke and Acts is still widely held: "This similarity is so strong that it is generally admitted to establish the fact that the two books in their present shape come from one author or editor, whatever materials he may have used in them."[31] Such linguistic similarities have been widely noted and need not be repeated here.[32]

Over a century ago, though, F. C. Blass commented on the differences in style between Luke and Acts: "Although it is also easily grasped from the diction that Luke himself is the author of both the Gospel and Acts, nevertheless, in the second book the end result is more Hellenic and certain additional words and particles are used, for example the particle τε, which, in addition to καί and δέ, usually connects final clauses in Acts. . . ."[33] And Hawkins's note in 1909 still rings true today, the work of Blass, Clark, et al., notwithstanding: "I do not know that much attention has been paid to the linguistic differences between the two."[34]

---

[30] Clark, *Acts of the Apostles;* Hawkins, *Horae Synopticae.*

[31] Hawkins, *Horae Synopticae,* 174.

[32] See ibid., 175–176.

[33] Blass, *Ed. phil.,* 18. The Latin quotation reads: "Ipse Lukas quamquam etiam ex dictione facile cognoscitur eundem et Evangelii et Actorum esse auctorem, tamen in hoc altero libro et ἑλληνικώτερος evasit et aliis quibusdam assuevit vocabulis vel particulis, velut τε particulae, quae iuxta καί et δέ in Actis demum sententias conectere solet."

[34] Hawkins, *Horae Synopticae,* 177. Hawkins categorizes the differences under five headings: (1) words and phrases characteristic of Luke's Gospel in contrast to the other Synoptics, but used in Acts at least three times as often in Luke (especially ἀνήρ, ἄχρι, ἐγένετο followed by infinitive, ὀνόματι, τε); (2) words and phrases never occurring in Luke, but frequently in Acts (see chart, 178); (3) words and phrases rarely occurring in Luke, but frequently in Acts (see chart, 179); (4) words and phrases frequently occurring in Luke, but never in Acts (see chart, 179); (5) words and phrases frequently occurring in Luke, but much more rarely in Acts. Clark goes over much of the same evidence, nuancing it

The standard reply to the work of Clark and others is to cite the work of W. L. Knox, but as Dawsey rightly points out,

> Knox's defense of the unified authorship of Luke and Acts was based on some presuppositions not generally held today by those who treat Luke-Acts as a narrative unity. For instance, Knox thought of the ancient writer as a very careless reviser who for the most part incorporated his sources verbatim. The changes which he made were occasional, Knox believed, and for the most part only attempts at improving the style of the sources. Far from thinking of Luke and Acts as two parts of the same writing, Knox thought that Acts itself was composed of two different documents, and Luke of several documents. He also assumed that the Gospel and Acts were written with different purposes in mind, and were read under different conditions. . . . It is enough to say that Knox defended the authorial unity of Luke and Acts by separating them.[35]

The purpose here is not to rehearse this evidence again, but to take up Dawsey's challenge and ask in what ways such explorations of Lukan vocabulary and style assist in understanding the similarities and differences in the narration of Luke and Acts from a narratological point of view. To do that, the narrative functions of the oft-noted δέ, καί, and τε *solitarium* in Acts will be examined and contrasted with Luke, and then some other differences in first-level narration will be noted. This is obviously no effort to be exhaustive, but rather is an attempt to demonstrate how the "old" vocabulary and stylistic evidence might be recast upon a narratological grid.[36]

In a recent study, Stephen Levinsohn has employed linguistic analysis to examine what he calls development units (DU) in

---

further by noting word frequency in Paul and the other Gospels, as well as Luke and Acts.

[35] Dawsey, "Literary Unity," 52. Dawsey also argues (ibid.), "This, by the way, seems also true of J. C. Hawkins, who accepted the tradition of single authorship, but only by postulating a long period of time between the writing of the two books."

[36] Perhaps these examples will prompt other examinations of the evidence presented by Clark, Hawkins, and Beck to determine its significance for understanding the narrative unity of Luke and Acts.

Acts.[37] In Part Two of his study, Levinsohn argues that "whenever *de* is used in the narrative of Acts, it introduces something distinctive."[38] More than 90 percent of the examples of δε can be accounted for by either a change of temporal setting or a real change in the underlying subject.[39] Likewise, Levinsohn finds a consistent pattern for the use of καί in Acts:

> Thus, *kai* is used for two different but related reasons in Acts. First, it introduces sentences in which nothing distinctive is presented. Second, it associates distinctive elements, when the information conveyed does not in fact develop the story. . . . The appearance of *kai* is not arbitrary, but relates to the overall structure and purpose of the book of Acts.[40]

The use of τε solitarium is likewise consistent in Acts. Τε solitarium is used in Acts either (1) to show a close affinity between the sentences it links (thus occuring within a DU rather than introducing a new one distinguishing it from the function of δε); or (2) to indicate that the sentences which it links are of unequal importance (distinguishing it from the function of καί).[41]

In each instance, Levinsohn marshalls impressive evidence from Acts for his assertions. What is interesting for the purposes of this volume is the appendix at the end of the volume entitled, "Development Units in the Gospel of Luke."[42] There Levinsohn compares his findings about Acts with Luke.[43] He first

---

[37] Levinsohn, *Textual Connections in Acts,* 179. Levinsohn defines a developmental unit as "one or more sentences of narrative, introduced by a developmental conjunction (e.g., *de*) and associated by *kai* or *te*, which presents a new development in the story" (p. 179).

[38] Ibid., 95.

[39] Levinsohn notes that in 263 occurrences of *de,* there is a change of subject. The other 44 instances of *de* where the subject is the same can be explained by one of several other factors of which each "in itself is enough to make distinctive the sentence in which it is present" (p. 90).

[40] Ibid., 120.

[41] Ibid., 122. See the examples cited by Levinsohn, ibid., 123–136.

[42] Ibid., 173–177.

[43] See also the extensive article by Levinsohn, "Notes on the Distribution of *de* and *kai* in the Narrative Framework of Luke's Gospel."

observes that "in many narrative sections of Luke's Gospel, *de* and *kai* are used in exactly the same way as in Acts."[44] But Levinsohn also notes some significant differences. First, he suggests that καί is often used to introduce the first sentence(s) of an incident or sub-incident in the Gospel of Luke which stands in sharp contrast to the pattern in Acts.[45] Second, he observes, "*Te* solitarium is not used in Luke's Gospel."[46] Finally, and perhaps most significantly, Levinsohn argues that the Third Gospel is a more episodic and less tightly woven narrative than is Acts.

> In the body of the narrative of Acts, every DU develops from the immediately preceding DU, or else begins the development of a further train of thought within the overall purpose of the book. This continuity of development is not a feature of all narratives. In particular, it is not a feature of Luke's Gospel.[47]

A number of reasons might be given to explain these differences in the use of conjunctions to connect and divide the narratives of Luke and Acts,[48] but one that remains essentially unexplored is that the narration of the discourse of these two narratives is distinct, a fact that is most clearly seen from the consistent function of conjunctions to provide textual connection in Acts that are significantly different from Luke. Levinsohn's study moves far beyond the old attempts to count word frequencies and attempts to account for the literary function of these conjunctions. If a distinctive pattern and function can be established in Acts for the use of what seem to be insignificant conjunctions and particles, then the narrative unity of Luke and Acts on the discourse level is by no means a foregone

[44] Ibid., 173.

[45] Ibid.

[46] Ibid., 174. He does suggest that καί ἐγένετο is a possible equivalent in the Gospel to τε in Acts.

[47] Ibid., 172. This may explain why Tannehill found it more congenial to follow the narrative sequence of Acts in his second volume while he organized the first volume around the relationship of Jesus to the other major characters (see above, n. 15).

[48] Levinsohn himself (p. 177) suggests that the fact that Jesus is the sole central character in the Gospel might account for lack of well-defined DU's.

conclusion.[49] Research of this nature may seem tedious, but it is a necessary prerequisite to the conclusion that Luke and Acts form a narrative unity.[50]

In addition to literary patterns which demonstrate the distinctiveness of the Lukan narratives,[51] the three literary techniques of Luke and Acts most often used to demonstrate their narrative unity, parallels, linkage, and the prefaces, also deserve attention.

1. Parallels. Parallels between Jesus and Paul, between Jesus and Peter, and between Jesus and Stephen have been cited for nearly a century.[52] For example, the trial of Paul before Festus and Agrippa II (Acts 25–26) parallels the appearance of Christ before Pilate and Herod Antipas (Luke 23). The healing of a lame man by Peter (Acts 3:1-10) parallels the healing of a lame man by Jesus (5:17-26) and by Paul (14:8-10).[53] The last words of Stephen parallel the last words of Jesus.[54]

Whether such parallels can demonstrate narrative unity, however, is another matter. Susan Praeder has helpfully distinguished between parallel composition which is "the realm of the author" and parallel reading which is "the realm of the reader."[55] Parallel composition, that is, apparently intentional similarities in

---

[49] This conclusion is strenghtened by another insight of Levinsohn. He asks the question "Can the book of Acts be treated as a single homogeneous entity, for the purposes of linguistic analysis?" After acknowledging that the author probably had several sources from which he drew, Levinsohn further notes, "The present author also finds no evidence of changes in the principles on which the order of words or the distribution of conjunctions are based, as the book progresses. Rather, examples of most phenomena can generally be found, whichever part of the book is examined."

[50] W. L. Knox remarked in this regard: "It may seem that to discuss such matters is to waste time over minute trivialities; but a man can be hanged for a finger-print"! (*Acts,* 2).

[51] Characterization is another area where differences emerge. See chapter 2. See also David Gowler (*Host, Guest, Enemy, Friend*), who argues that characterization in Luke is substantially different from Acts.

[52] For a history of research, see Gasque, *Acts,* 21–54; Talbert, *Literary Patterns;* Mark Powell, *What is Narrative Criticism?;* and Susan Praeder, "Jesus-Paul."

[53] See also the parallel between Luke 7:11-17 and Acts 9:36-43.

[54] For other parallels, see Powell and Talbert (above, n. 52).

[55] Susan M. Praeder, "Jesus-Paul," 39.

content, language, literary form, sequence, structure, or theme in two or more places, may point to a close literary relationship between two texts. It does not, however, require the conclusion that the two texts must be a single, continuous work.[56]

Parallel reading involves "selective reading, remembering and forgetting, looking backward and forward in the text and to other texts, and long and painstaking reading."[57] While Praeder acknowledges several contributions of parallel reading, she fails to observe that such parallel reading seems to rest on the assumption of the authorial unity of Luke and Acts.[58] In fact, one could show striking parallels between Acts and other of the Synoptic Gospels if one were convinced that the same author wrote Mark and Acts.

Furthermore, closer scrutiny shows some alleged parallels to function very differently in the two narratives. "Journeys" are a good example. Scholars have often noted the parallels between the journey of Jesus in Luke and the journeys of the apostles, especially Paul, in Acts.[59] In Luke, the didactic material embedded in the narrative of Jesus' journey to Jerusalem serves to heighten the tension of the journey to the city where they kill prophets (13:33).[60] Like the Queen in *Alice in Wonderland,* Jesus seems to be running as fast as he can just to stay where he is!

Retardation, that is, delaying the narration of the next event, is a common device for stimulating reader interest.[61] Such delays occur frequently in the Gospel (as in the travel accounts) and

---

[56] Ibid., 29.

[57] Ibid., 38.

[58] One wonders what kind of "Johannine reading" of Acts could be assembled if Irenaeus had credited John, not Luke, with penning Acts!

[59] See Pervo, *Profit with Delight,* 50: "Although travel constitutes the structural basis for both Luke and Acts, the theme functions differently in the two works. Acts' journeys may be traced on a map, as every Sunday-school child knows. This is not true of Jesus' journey to Jerusalem (Luke 9:51 – 19:44). In the Gospel the journey is devoted to the teaching of Jesus. Apostolic adventures fill the pages of Acts. Sources alone cannot explain the problem . . ." See also above, 37–40.

[60] For an extended discussion of the function of the "travel narrative" in the plot of the Third Gospel, see Parsons, *The Departure of Jesus,* 91–93.

[61] Rimmon-Kenan, *Narrative Fiction,* 126; see also Genette, *Narrative Time.*

seem to be a major focus here in Luke in order to educate the reader. Journeys are important to the plot of Acts, but for a much different reason. Richard Pervo has correctly observed: "Contrast with the Gospel indicates that the travels reported in Acts seek not so much to teach as to describe in an exciting way the experiences of Paul and his predecessors."[62] The journeys in Luke and Acts, then, are parallel in structure but certainly not in function.

2. Linkage. From a narratological point of view, linkage is the literary strategy which "links the novel not to its own beginning and middle, but to the body of another, often as yet unwritten, novel."[63] However, such linkage is not a recent narrative strategy. Lucian of Samosa suggested the principle of interlacing events (συμπεριπλοχῇ τῶν πραγματῶν).[64] Linkage or interlacing has long been noted as a significant sign of the interrelatedness of Luke and Acts.[65] The most obvious linkage between Luke and Acts is the preface of Acts which refers both to "Theophilus" and to the "first word" (πρῶτον λόγον). But here it should be noted that the reference to the "first book" in Acts 1 not only unites the two works; it is also evidence that for the implied author (if not for his subsequent readers) the second volume was clearly distinguishable from the first, a point often overlooked in discussions of the preface.

Other links exist: the departure of Jesus recorded in Luke 24:50-53 and Acts 1:5-11; Jesus' command that the disciples "stay in the city until endowed with power from on high" (24:49; see Acts 2); his commission that the disciples should preach "repentance and forgiveness of sins" (24:47; see Acts 2:38; 3:19; 5:31); and his reference to "witnesses" (24:48; see Acts 1:8, 22; 2:32; 3:15; 4:33). In addition to these links between Luke 24 and Acts 1,

[62] Pervo, *Profit with Delight,* 56.

[63] Torgovnick, *Closure,* 15.

[64] *How to Write History,* 52–54, 63–64; cited by J. Dupont, "La Question du plan des Actes des Apôtres," 220–231.

[65] See J. G. Davies, "The Prefiguration of the Ascension" 229–230; Charles H. Talbert, *Literary Patterns; Dupont,* "La Question du plan des Actes des Apôtres," 220–231. For further bibliography, see Talbert, *Literary Patterns,* 58f.

there are also the similarities between the transfiguration in Luke 9 and Acts 1 (the "cloud"; the "mountain").[66] Finally, the phrase "and behold two men" (καὶ ἰδοὺ ἄνδρες δύο) is one example of an exact verbal correspondence which links the transfiguration, resurrection, and ascension narratives (see Luke 9:30; 24:4; Acts 1:10).

In the light of these examples of linkage, two points should be noted. First despite such strong linkage, important gaps between the two narratives exist. One of the strongest links between Luke and Acts is the repetition of the ascension narrative. But that repetition is not without significant variations (forty days later, two angels present, dialogue). Even the suggestion that the variations may be explained in literary terms — Luke 24:50-53 functions as an ending to bring proper closure to the Gospel, and Acts 1:5-11 is a narrative beginning designed to provide entry into the narrative world — suggests that we have here two independent, discrete narratives, at least on the discourse level.[67] More interesting is the saying of Jesus in Acts 20:35 which is linked to the story of Jesus but finds no correspondence in Luke's Gospel.[68] Further, the quotation of John the Baptist in Acts 13:25 is closer in language to John than to Luke![69] The point here is that neither parallelism nor linkage provides conclusive evidence that Luke and Acts form one narrative on the discourse level. Rather the ambiguous evidence, if anything, points toward their independence.

3. Lukan Prefaces. Perhaps the linchpin to any argument for Lukan unity is the evidence of the prefaces. In support of his view that the Lukan corpus was a "single, continuous work,"

[66] Davies, "The Prefigurement of the Ascension," saw no less than fourteen points of contact between these two chapters; Talbert pared that list down to three.

[67] This was the conclusion Parsons reached at the end of *The Departure of Jesus in Luke-Acts,* 198–199.

[68] This "agraphon" is unique to Acts.

[69] Compare, e.g., the use of ἄξιος in Acts 13:25 and John 1:27 (ἱκανός is found in Luke, Mark, and Matthew). Note the textual problem in John 1:27 where Mss. p[66] and p[75] replace ἄξιος with ἱκανός.

Cadbury claimed that Luke 1:1-4 was "the real preface to Acts as well as to the Gospel, written by the author when he contemplated not merely one but both volumes."[70] Cadbury supported his argument by reminding the reader that

> it was the custom in antiquity, on account of the purely physical conditions of writing, to divide works into volumes, to prefix to the first a preface for the whole, and to add secondary prefaces to the beginning of each later one. . . . The book of Acts is no afterthought.[71]

In a very uncharacteristic fashion, Cadbury cited little evidence from primary literature for this "custom in antiquity," and much subsequent scholarship has also failed to produce it.[72] Those who accept the contention that Luke 1:1-4 serves as a preface to both volumes usually cite Josephus' *Against Apion* as "a two-volume work with primary and secondary prefaces very similar to those of Luke-Acts."[73] Indeed, the similarities are impressive:

In my history of Antiquities, most excellent Epaphroditus, I have, I think, made sufficiently clear to any who may peruse that work the extreme antiquity of our Jewish race. . . . Since, however, I observe that a considerable number of persons, influenced by the malicious calumnies of certain individuals, discredit the statements in my history concerning our antiquity. . . . I consider it my duty to devote a brief treatise to all these points; in order at once to convict our detractors of malig-	Inasmuch as many have undertaken to compile a narrative of the things which have been accomplished among us, just as they were delivered to us by those who from the beginning were eyewitnesses and ministers of the word, it seemed good to me also, having followed all things closely for some time past, to write an orderly account for you, most excellent Theophilus, that you may know the truth concerning the things of which you have been informed (Luke 1:1-4).

[70] Cadbury, "Commentary on the Preface of Luke," *Beginnings,* Appendix C, 2:492.

[71] Ibid., 491.

[72] Contra Cadbury, Haenchen, Schürmann, Nolland, Dillon, S. Brown.

[73] David Aune, *The New Testament in Its Literary Environment,* 121. See also Donald Juel, *Luke-Acts,* 10–12.

nity and deliberate falsehood, to correct the ignorance of others, and to instruct all who desire to know the truth concerning the antiquity of our race (*Against Apion*, I.1).

In the first volume of this work, my most esteemed Epaphroditus, I demonstrated the antiquity of our race. . . . I shall now proceed to refute the rest of the authors who have attacked us (*Against Apion*, II.1).

In the first book, O Theophilus, I have dealt with all that Jesus began to do and teach, until the day when he was taken up, after he had given commandment through the Holy Spirit to the apostles whom he had chosen (Acts 1:1-2).

Equally interesting, however, is a comparison of the ways Luke and the first volume of *Against Apion* end:

This book, however, having already run to a suitable length, I propose at this point to begin a second, in which I shall endeavour to supply the remaining portion of my subject (*Against Apion*, I.322–25).[74]

Then he led them out as far as Bethany, and lifting up his hands he blessed them. While he blessed them, he departed from them [and was carried up into heaven]. And they [worshipped him and] returned to Jerusalem with great joy, and were continually in the temple blessing God (Luke 24:50-53).

Josephus here clearly anticipated continuing his work, but Lukas shows no indication of contemplating a second volume. Lukas does not mark the end of the book with any sort of marker or device to indicate to the reader that the end of volume 1 (Luke) has arrived. Rather, he goes to great lengths to provide a sense of closure to this story about Jesus.[75]

[74] The Greek text reads: Ἀλλ' ἐπειδὴ σύμμετρον ἤδη τὸ βιβλίον εἴληφε μέγεθος, ἑτέραν ποιησάμενος ἀρχὴν τὰ λοιπὰ τῶν εἰς τὸ προκείμενον πειράσομαι προσαποδοῦναι.
[75] For a detailed argument of this point, see Parsons, *The Departure of Jesus in Luke-Acts*.

Others, like Charles Talbert, who argue that Luke and Acts share a biographical mold, prefer comparing the preface of Acts to that of volume II of Philo's *Life of Moses*.[76] Again the parallels are interesting:

The former treatise (προτέρα σύνταξις) dealt with the birth and nurture of Moses; also with his education and career as a ruler, in which capacity his conduct was not merely blameless but highly praiseworthy; also with the works which he performed in Egypt and during the journeys both at the Red Sea and in the wilderness. . . . The present treatise is concerned with matters allied and consequent to these (Philo, *Life of Moses*, II.1. 1).	In the first book, O Theophilus, I have dealt with all that Jesus began to do and teach, until the day when he was taken up, after he had given commandment through the Holy Spirit to the apostles whom he had chosen (Acts 1:1-2).

Again, however, the end of volume one of the *Life of Moses* stands in sharp contrast to the end of Luke:

We have now told the story of Moses' actions in his capacity of king. We must next deal with all that he achieved by his powers as high priest and legislator, powers which he possessed as the most fitting accompaniments of kingship (Philo, *Life of Moses*, I.334).	Then he led them out as far as Bethany, and lifting up his hands he blessed them. While he blessed them, he departed from them [and was carried up into heaven]. And they [worshiped him and] returned to Jerusalem with great joy, and were continually in the temple blessing God (Luke 24:50-53).

Textually embedded in the *Life of Moses* is Philo's reference to a second volume which is an obvious continuation of the first. The Gospel of Luke avoids such explicit references to a second volume. Some proleptic statements in Luke ultimately do find

---

[76] Talbert, *Reading Luke*, 11.

fulfillment in Acts (e.g., the promise to the disciples that "they will be enclothed with power from on high" Luke 24:47; see Acts 2).[77] That unfulfilled proleptic statements, however, *require* a subsequent volume cannot be substantiated. One need only consider the prolepsis in Mark 16:5 where the young man tells the women to inform the disciples that Jesus is "going before them into Galilee." This promise remains unfulfilled at 16:8, yet no one has proposed a second volume to the Gospel of Mark.[78] Cadbury has not sufficiently documented his contention, nor have those who follow his views, and the prefaces neither prove nor disprove the unity of Luke and Acts.

Cadbury disregarded the notion that Acts was a kind of sequel as the false impression of the modern reader: "The impression made on the English reader by Acts i.1, that the author is making a new start or at least preparing a kind of sequel to his gospel, would not occur to an early reader."[79] Elsewhere he commented: "Occasionally, no doubt, independent works were addressed to the same patron and referred to one another in terms similar to the examples we have given, but without specific knowledge to that effect the presumption in such cases is that the two volumes are really a single work."[80]

Despite Cadbury's caveat, other scholars have labeled Acts as a "sequel" to Luke.[81] Joseph Fitzmyer writes: "There is the unique aspect of the Lucan Gospel, in that it alone is fitted in the New Testament with a sequel—and with a sequel that has its own literary, didactic, apologetic, geographical, historical, and theological perspectives."[82] That Lukas had access to other models

[77] On prolepses, see Gérard Genette, *Narrative Discourse.*

[78] Interestingly, of course, someone did write a conclusion to Mark (16:9-20) which included the fulfillment of the promised Galilean appearance. See further comments on this passage, p. 86.

[79] Cadbury, *Beginnings,* 2:491.

[80] Cadbury, *Making,* 9.

[81] Haenchen (*Acts,* 97) called Acts a "sequel" to the Gospel, but he did not define the term and did not seek parallels in Luke's literary environment. Even before Cadbury's work, C. C. Torrey (*The Composition and Date of Acts,* 59) had referred to Acts as a "sequel" to Luke.

[82] Fitzmyer, *Gospel according to Luke,* 1:3. Elsewhere Fitzmyer makes it clear that Luke and Acts form a two-volume work and he is inclined to treat the

which used sequel(s) to a first volume is a point already made in the previous chapter.

Extent of Participation in the Story

Rimmon-Kenan further distinguishes between narrators in terms of their participation in the story. A *heterodiegetic* narrator is one "who does not participate in the story," whereas a *homodiegetic* narrator "takes part in it at least in some manifestation of his 'self.'"[83] Extradiegetic narrators, like the narrators of Luke and Acts (see previous section), can be either heterodiegetic or homodiegetic. Narrators who are both extradiegetic and heterodiegetic contribute to narratorial authority or "omniscience."[84]

Excluding the Gospel prologue which does contain first-person narration, the extradiegetic narrator of Luke is also exclusively heterodiegetic, that is, he does not directly participate in the story.[85] Meir Sternberg has been critical of the shift in the Gospel's narration from an obtrusive, *telling* first-person narrator with limited knowledge in the prologue to an unobtrusive, *showing* third-person narrator who is anonymous and omniscient in the subsequent narrative:[86]

---

two works together, blurring any distinctions that might exist between the two (ibid., 1.vii).

[83] Rimmon-Kenan, *Narrative Fiction*, 95.

[84] Ibid. Omniscience, according to Rimmon-Kenan, is communicated through several techniques: familiarity with the characters' inmost thoughts and emotions; knowledge of past, present, and future, observation of events in which the characters are presumably alone, and knowledge of events which occur simultaneously in different locations.

[85] Masculine pronouns are used consistently when referring to the narrator. While the sex of the narrator of Luke and Acts cannot be definitively established, Susan Lanser (*The Narrative Act*, 16) has persuasively argued that "writers and narrators are presumed male unless the text offers a marking to the contrary." This statement would seem especially true of the biblical narratives which reflect, in varying degrees, a patriarchal point of view.

[86] On the distinction between *showing* and *telling*, see Wayne Booth, *The Rhetoric of Fiction*, 3–20.

But his practice flatly contradicts his empirical undertaking and terms of reference [in the prologue]. The angel's apparition to Zechariah, the interior monologues of various characters, Jesus' prayer on the Mount of Olives while the disciples are asleep: all these form events accessible only by the privilege of omniscience which Luke virtually disclaims.[87]

However, the extradiegetic narrator of the prefaces is not the narrator, *sensu strictissimo* (in the strictest sense) of the text precisely because he is not omnipotent, etc.[88] The use of first-person narration in the Gospel prologue is, as has been argued elsewhere, a framing device and is a conventional pattern in much ancient literature.[89] In Acts, the narrator occasionally functions as a homodiegetic narrator—he is an active participant in the story he tells. This is the problem of first-person narration in Acts. Here, the narrator does intrude into the narrative in the so-called "we" passages (16:10-17; 20:5-15; 21:1-18; and 27:1—28:16). The narrator chooses a course of action in telling his story in Acts which is distinct from that in Luke.

Further, it is doubtful that the first person of the Gospel prologue refers to the same group as the "we" in Acts. William Kurz has commented: "In Acts, the 'I' never sets himself apart or distinguishes himself from the 'We' to act or react individually, as he does in the prologue in describing his personal writing on behalf of the 'We.'"[90] The narrator who intrudes as a participant in the narrative is unique to Acts and separates the narrator of Acts from the Gospel narrator.[91]

---

[87] Meir Sternberg, *The Poetics of Biblical Narrative*, 86. This reveals the dissonance between "Luke the Historian" who writes a conventional preface and the narrator who functions much like a modern novelist.

[88] Sternberg's comment inadvertently points out the problem of determining genre(s) from the prefaces.

[89] See Parsons, *The Departure of Jesus in Luke-Acts*, 97.

[90] Kurz, "Narrative Approaches to Luke-Acts," 210. Kurz is optimistic about the potential contribution narrative analysis makes to the solution of the problematic "we" passages. See, however, Susan M. Praeder ("The Problem of First Person Narration," 193–218) who has made a strong case for the view that source, redaction, and comparative literary analyses do not fully explicate the "we" passages in Acts.

[91] The use of the first-person plural tends to be quite late: John 21; 2 Peter

On the second level of the narrative, intradiegetic narrators may likewise be either heterodiegetic or homodiegetic. Again, the narratives of Luke and Acts are distinct. In Luke, Jesus is an intra-heterodiegetic narrator, that is, in the stories he narrates — the parables — he does not appear as a character. In Acts, on the other hand, Paul twice narrates his conversion experience (22:3-21; 26:9-20; cf. 9:1-29). In so doing, he functions like intra-homodiegetic narrators "who narrate stories in which they also participate as characters."[92] Again, the examination of the extent of participation by the narrator in the story indicates that the narrative voices in Luke and Acts function differently at the level of discourse.

Degree of Perceptibility

The degree of perceptibility, according to Rimmon-Kenan, "ranges from the maximum of covertness (often mistaken for a complete absence of a narrator) to the maximum of overtness."[93] She discusses signs of the narrator's presence in "mounting order of perceptibility" which range from the description of setting, the identification of characters, temporal summary, definition of character, reports of what characters did not think or say, and commentary.[94] This "laundry list" serves as a convenient framework for comparing the perceptibility of the narrator of Luke with the narrator of Acts.[95]

(both second century); not to mention the *Gospel of Peter,* and a host of Christian apocryphal texts.

[92] The three accounts of Paul's conversion present the best example because they are extended stories. Acts 22:3-21, in fact, contains the interaction of three characters, making it roughly analogous to Jesus' "narrative parables." Note also Acts 10 where both Cornelius and Peter function as intra-homodiegetic narrators, although the "stories" are much briefer.

[93] Rimmon-Kenan, *Narrative Fiction,* 96.

[94] Ibid. Rimmon-Kenan is here borrowing from the list of Seymour Chatman, *Story and Discourse,* 220–252.

[95] These categories overlap in several instances, as Rimmon-Kenan acknowledges. Hence, the same episode or description may be used as illustrative of more than one of these categories.

1. Description of Setting. Rimmon-Kenan admits that a narrator's description of the setting is a "relatively minimal sign of a narrator's presence."[96] It is difficult to distinguish Luke's narrator from the narrator of Acts on this basis. It is likewise difficult to distinguish any Gospel narrator on the basis of the description of settings.[97] Nonetheless, certain settings familiar in the Gospel are absent in Acts. The conflict scenes set in the home of a Pharisee, so prominent in Luke (7:36-50; 11:37-54; 14:1-24), are missing in Acts. In one instance the same setting receives different descriptions. According to Acts, the Mount of Olives is located "a sabbath day's journey away" from Jerusalem (1:12). This is the only reference to the Mount of Olives in Acts. Although the narrator of Luke mentions the Mount of Olives several times (19:27, 37; 21:37), he never locates it in reference to Jerusalem. If Luke and Acts are united at the level of discourse, one would expect such a description to be given in the first occurrence in Luke 19:29.

This spatial location could also be construed to suggest that not only are the narrators of Luke and Acts distinct, but so are the narratees even though both are called "Theophilus." The narratee of Acts presumably knows the distance from the Mount of Olives to Jerusalem; Luke's Theophilus does not.[98] As Rimmon-Kenan has argued: "Such statements also imply an assumption that the narratee-reader does not share this knowledge, an assumption which characterizes one of the narrator's roles, i.e. to communicate to others what they don't know."[99]

---

[96] Rimmon-Kenan, *Narrative Fiction,* 96–97.

[97] Note, however, that in Mark conflict between Jesus and the religious authorities always occurs in a public setting—a pattern not found in Luke or Acts. See Rhoads and Michie, *Mark as Story,* 67.

[98] See Culpepper's discussion of narratee in *Anatomy of the Fourth Gospel.* Interestingly, just as the implied author for Luke and Acts is the same but the narrators are distinct, so the implied reader of Luke and Acts is the same "Theophilus." The narratees, however, are different in terms of the information they possess, the languages they know, etc.

[99] Rimmon-Kenan, *Narrative Fiction,* 97. Rimmon-Kenan is here referring to the identification of characters, but her words apply equally well to the description of setting.

2. Identification of characters. Identifying characters, Rimmon-Kenan argues, shows "prior 'knowledge' of the character on the part of the narrator who can therefore identify the former to the reader at the very beginning of the text."[100] Both Luke and Acts provide commentary on certain characters. Whereas both narrators tend to use similar techniques in the identification of characters, in several instances, the narrator of Acts does use some unique techniques to identify certain characters.[101]

The narrator of Acts translates the names of characters as a means of identifying them. This technique conforms to Greek practice, and the fact that the Third Gospel does not employ it is another point of differentiation. For example, Luke 8:54 presumably omits the Aramaic phrase, *Talitha cumi,* and its translation found in Mark 5:41. In Acts, the narrator is willing to exploit this technique in two cases.[102] The narrator glosses "Barnabas" as "Son of encouragement" (= "one who encourages," 4:36). In actual fact this is wrong. The name may be theophoric ("Son of Nebo," a pagan deity), but it does reflect the role Barnabas will play in Acts, for, as Sheeley has observed: "Each time the reader encounters Barnabas in the narrative, Barnabas is living up to his name by encouraging or exhorting those around him."[103] Barnabas is the son of encouragement both by identification and characterization — both of which are the creation of the narrator.

Likewise, the reader will be hard-pressed to make etymological connections between the name of Elymas and the narrator's translation of it as "magician" ("for that is the meaning of his name" 13:8). Sheeley suggested: "Elymas seems to have been translated as 'magician' in order to highlight the triumph of Paul

---

[100] Ibid.

[101] See Steven M. Sheeley, "Narrative Asides and Narrative Authority," 11–13; idem, *Narrative Asides in Luke-Acts.*

[102] A third translation actually seems to have an etymological relationship to the name it translates. In 9:36, we read: "Now there was at Joppa a disciple named Tabitha, which means Dorcas." The Aramaic word "Tabitha" and the Greek name "Dorcas" both mean *gazelle.*

[103] Sheeley, "Narrative Asides and Narrative Authority," 12.

over magic."[104] The narrator of Luke, on the other hand, does not gloss, for example, the name "Jesus," although that character is very important (cf. Matt 1:23). Again, the narrator of Acts, in contrast to Luke, uses the translation of a name as a way of further identifying a character, and presumably providing information unavailable to the narratee, ostensibly because in the cases of Barnabas, and Elymas, the narratee does not know Aramaic.[105] The translations are quite wrong, pseudo-scholarship being pressed into the service of characterization.

3. Temporal Summary. Rimmon-Kenan noted that "summary presupposes a desire to account for time-passage, to satisfy questions in a narratee's mind about what has happened in the interval. An account cannot but draw attention to the one who felt obliged to make such an account."[106] Little comment is necessary to add to the long-noted observation that summaries are far more prominent as a literary convention in Acts than in Luke.[107] Short summaries (1:14; 6:7; 9:31-32) are coupled with longer summaries (2:42-47; 4:32-35; 5:12-16) to move the story line along. Luke is not devoid of such summary statements (see 4:14), but certainly the narrator of Acts has employed them more extensively. Close study of these summary statements not only "impl[ies] the presence of a narrator," according to Rimmon-Kenan, but also "his notion of what should be told in detail and what could be narrated with greater conciseness."[108] A much better sense of what is essential and what is extraneous is gleaned from the summaries in Acts, which function as transitional units from one episode to the next.

---

[104] Ibid. See also Susan Garrett, *Demise of the Devil.*

[105] This technique conforms to Greek practice, and the fact that the Third Gospel does not employ it is another point of differentiation.

[106] Rimmon-Kenan, *Narrative Fiction,* 97. Rimmon-Kenan is quoting Chatman, *Story and Discourse,* 223.

[107] See Cadbury, "The Summaries in Acts" in *Beginnings,* 5:392–402; also Pierre Benoit, "Some notes on the 'Summaries' in Acts 2, 4, and 5," 95–103.

[108] Rimmon-Kenan, *Narrative Fiction,* 98.

4. Definition of character. The difference between the identification of characters (2 above) and the definition of characters is important in Rimmon-Kenan's discussion. She argues: "Whereas an identification of a character implies only the narrator's prior knowledge about or acquaintance with him, definition also suggests an abstraction, generalization or summing up on the part of the narrator as well as a desire to present such labelling as authoritative characterization."[109] Identification in both Luke and Acts is limited to descriptive phrases (see above, p. 000). For example, in Acts, we are told that a certain Joseph, a nominee for Judas's replacement, was "called Barsabbas, who was surnamed Justus" (1:23). When those comments lead the reader to hold a positive or negative opinion of a certain character, the narrator has moved beyond the descriptive function.[110] In Luke, for example, Joseph of Arimathea is described as "a member of the council, a good and righteous man, who had not consented to their purpose and deed, and he was looking for the kingdom of God" (23:50-51). The narrator obviously wishes the reader to reach a positive value judgment about Joseph, a view reinforced by the story of the burial of Jesus which follows. Similarly, in Acts, Cornelius is described in a most positive way as "a devout man who feared God with all his household, gave alms liberally to people, and prayed constantly to God" (10:2). Again, the narrator leads the reader to form a positive assessment of the centurion, Cornelius. In both cases, the narrator introduces an individual whose position (member of the Sanhedrin, Roman officer) might suggest a hostile stance toward Jesus or Judaism in a way that blocks such assumptions by the reader and provides instead a positive orientation toward each. Both Luke and Acts use this technique of narrative intervention to prevent undesired assumptions.

Definition of characters may also refer to characterization which is extended over the entire narrative. The Lukan point

[109] Ibid.
[110] In this sense, Barnabas as "son of encouragement" may also be an example of "definition of character."

of view on the various characters who appear in both narratives — especially the disciples and Jewish leaders — merits further consideration, but there is evidence that the narrators depict the same group in different ways in the two narratives. For instance, those who will find differences in Luke and Acts recall the more favorable characterization of the Jewish populace in the Gospel than is presented in Acts.

5. Reports of what characters did not think or say. "A narrator who can tell things of which the characters are either unconscious or which they deliberately conceal is clearly felt as an independent source of information."[111] "Inside views" in both Luke and Acts, for the most part, lack depth and frequency. Still, there are noteworthy differences. The narrator of Luke does know the unconscious deliberations of his characters (see Table 1).

Table 1
Inside Views of Luke's Narrator

Verse	Quotation	Referent(s)
19:11	"They supposed the kingdom of God was to appear immediately"	crowd at Zacchaeus's house
22:61	"And Peter remembered the word of the Lord"	Peter
24:8	"And they remembered his words"	women at tomb
24:28	"But he pretended to be going further"	Jesus
24:37	"But they were startled and frightened and supposed that they saw a spirit"	Disciples

In Luke, however, the ability to discern what characters think or feel is shared by the narrator with the single omniscient

---

[111] Rimmon-Kenan, *Narrative Fiction,* 98.

protagonist, Jesus, who on several occasions knows the thoughts of friend and foe (see Table 2).

Table 2
Inside Views of Jesus in Luke

Verse	Quotation	Referent(s)
5:22	"When Jesus perceived their questionings, he answered them, 'Why do you question in your hearts?'"	Scribes/Pharisees
6:8	"But he knew their thoughts"	Scribes/Pharisees
9:47	"But when Jesus perceived the thought of their hearts"	Disciples
11:17	"But he, knowing their thoughts"	'some of the people'
24:38	"And he said to them, 'Why are you troubled, and why do questionings arise in your hearts?'"	Disciples

In Acts, the narrator presents several protagonists, e.g., Peter and Paul, who are not typically omniscient. Paul and Peter gain foreknowledge of certain events, but such knowledge often comes through visions (e.g., Peter's vision, chap. 10; Paul's vision, chap. 16). It is not enough to explain this lack of omniscience in the apostles by saying that Jesus is unique, since the apostles do perform miracles.[112] Still, the narrator is the only one in Acts who

Table 3
Inside Views of Acts' Narrator

Verse	Quotation	Referent(s)
12:9	"he thought he was seeing a vision"	Peter
21:29	"they supposed that Paul had brought him into the temple"[113]	Jews from Asia

[112] See our comments on this subject in chapter 4.

[113] See also Acts 5:5, 11; 6:5; 10:45; 12:16. The difficulty in deciding what qualifies as an inside view illustrates the unremarkable depth of the insights on the part of the narrator.

provides the "inside views" (see Table 3). And one should note that the "inside" views are even less penetrating than those of Luke. Although inside views are not prominent in either narrative, Luke does exhibit more varied use of this technique, especially through the character of Jesus.

6. Commentary. "Commentary can be either on the story or on the narration."[114] Commentary on the story may take the form of interpretation, judgments, or generalizations. Commentary is employed in both Luke and Acts and reveals a great deal about each respective narrator.[115]

i) Interpretation. "Interpretations often provide information not only about their direct object but also about the interpreter."[116] One of the most common forms of interpretation in both Luke and Acts is the use of narrative asides. Narrative asides are "parenthetical remarks addressed directly to the reader which interrupt the logical progression of the story."[117] Asides function similarly in Luke and Acts in several ways. (a) Self-conscious narration is found in both prefaces (Luke 1:1-4; Acts 1:1-5); (b) Both narrators in one or two instances provide general information which lies outside the storyworld. In the midst of telling the story of Jesus' passion, Luke's narrator pauses to append this note about Herod and Pilate who "became friends with each other that very day, for before this they had been at enmity with each other" (23:12). In Acts it is reported in an aside that Antioch was where "the disciples were for the first time called Christians" (11:26).[118] Such general information is of interest to the readers, reminding them that the narrator is privy to information which lies beyond the story-line at hand. (c) In most

---

[114] Rimmon-Kenan, *Narrative Fiction,* 98.
[115] We are indebted to Steven M. Sheeley ("Narrative Asides and Narrative Authority") for this section on commentary.
[116] Rimmon-Kenan, *Narrative Fiction,* 99.
[117] Sheeley, "Narrative Asides and Narrative Authority," 2.
[118] Sheeley's category of "inside views" has already been dealt with above (pp. 73–74).

cases, asides are used to provide information necessary for the readers to understand the story. The narrators of both Luke and Acts use asides in this way (Luke 2:22-23; 8:29; 9:14; Acts 1:15; 4:22; 5:17; 8:26; 23:8; 27:37).

Several differences in the way Luke and Acts use asides for interpretation do exist. Although Luke frequently employs narrative asides specifically for the purpose of identifying persons or places that may be unfamiliar to the reader (Luke 2:2, 4; 17:16; 20:27; 22:1; 23:18-19; 23:50-51), only once does the narrator of Acts use a narrative aside for such a purpose (6:9).[119] Sheeley has further noted, "In two places the narrator of Luke's Gospel precedes a parable of Jesus with an interpretative statement governing the way in which the parable is to be understood."[120] In Luke 14:7, a parable is preceded by this aside: "Now he told a parable to those who were invited, *when he marked how they chose the places of honor. . . .*" Before Jesus tells the parable of the widow and the judge, the narrator comments: "And he told them a parable, *to the effect that they ought always to pray and not lose heart*" (18:1). The effect of the commentary in both instances is to shape the interpretation which the reader gives to otherwise rather ambiguous parables. Such use of interpretation is more prominent in Luke.

While a number of the asides in Acts resemble or recall the narrative of the Third Gospel (see e.g., Acts 23:8), others function in a rather unique way in Acts: (a) As noted, the narrator of Acts pays close attention to the translation of foreign names, often pressing etymological connections for interpretive purposes (see above, pp. 69–70); (b) The narrator of Acts also provides details which seem extraneous to the story. On several occasions, the narrator takes time to mention the number of persons

---

[119] Ibid., 6. Cf. Acts 18:6. Sometimes in Luke, this information is withheld until the end of the story for greater impact on the reader. Hence, not until the leper has returned to thank Jesus does the narrator note, "Now he was a Samaritan" (17:16). And not until the child Jesus is born and placed in a manger is the reader told that "there was no room for them in the inn" (2:7).
[120] Ibid., 7.

present in attendance (1:15; 27:37) — giving details which seem extraneous to the story but which probably "lend a sense of verisimilitude to the narrative and provide the sort of detail which is the mark of a careful and thorough researcher."[121] The need to convince the reader of his reliability along with a desire to make his narrative entertaining explain the inclination of Acts' narrator to provide added and sometimes seemingly extraneous details.

ii) Judgments and Generalizations.[122] Rimmon-Kenan notes that judgments are "perhaps more revealing of the narrator's moral stand."[123] In addition to the positive assessments the narrators render about certain individuals like Joseph of Arimathea and Cornelius, negative evaluations are also offered. In at least one instance — the case of the Sadducees — it is difficult to distinguish between the judgment of Luke and Acts. In Luke 20:27 the narrator adds this judgment: "There came to him some Sadducees, *those who say that there is no resurrection.*" The Sadducees then use the hypothetical (from their point of view, impossible) case of a woman who had been married to seven brothers and ask Jesus the question, *"In the resurrection,* therefore, whose wife will the woman be?" (20:33). Within the Christian framework in which Luke writes, the reference to the Sadducees' denial of the resurrection is clearly perjorative. In Acts, this judgment upon the Sadducees is amplified and set in contrast with the Pharisees: "For the Sadducees say there is *no resurrection, nor angel, nor spirit;* but the Pharisees acknowledge them all" (23:8). The judgment is more severe in Acts where angels and spirits are added to the list of the Sadducees' skepticism. Again, this description must be viewed as perjorative from the narrator's point of view, since angels now regularly populate the narrative world of Acts and especially since the narrator has described the angelic deliverance of Peter from prison (12:6-11). Still, such variation in judgment on the Sadducees by the Lukan narrators is subtle and resists hard and fast conclusions. It should be noted, on

[121] Ibid., 11.
[122] Here two of Rimmon-Kenan's categories are combined into one.
[123] Rimmon-Kenan, *Narrative Fiction,* 99.

the other hand, that the narrator's positive evaluation of the Pharisees is sustained more consistently in Acts than in Luke, indicating that value judgments do, in some cases, differ between the narrators.[124]

The Implied Author(s) of Luke and Acts

Literary theory has, of course, emphasized the problem of identifying an implied author with a real historical author. The term "implied author" is, in Rimmon-Kenan's words, as "a construct inferred and assembled by the reader from all the components of the text" and "is best considered as a set of implicit norms rather than as a speaker or a voice (i.e. a subject)."[125] The implied author, according to Chatman, is "the principle that invented the narrator, along with everything else in the narrative, that stacked the cards in this particular way."[126] In other words, the implied author is responsible for the overall design of the narrative. And as Chatman further comments, "We can grasp the notion of implied author most clearly by comparing different narratives written by the same real author but presupposing different implied authors."[127] Again, there is at this level a clear distinction between the overall design of Luke and Acts that would justify keeping clear the distinctions between real author, implied author, and narrator, at least for Luke and Acts, despite practices to the contrary.

In terms of overall design, a reluctance in Luke to repeat material is matched by a propensity for such repetition in Acts.[128] In several instances, events from Luke's Gospel are repeated in

[124] This point has been made most recently and forcefully by David Gowler in *Host, Guest, Enemy, Friend.*

[125] Rimmon-Kenan, *Narrative Fiction,* 87, 88. She distinguishes her definition from that of Booth and Chatman.

[126] Chatman, *Story and Discourse,* 148.

[127] Ibid.

[128] Ironically, this distinction between Luke and Acts was first noticed by Henry Cadbury, champion of Lukan unity in one of his last writings on Luke-Acts, "Four Features of Lucan Style," 87–102.

Acts: the farewell scene of Jesus (Luke 24; Acts 1); the list of disciples (Luke 6:13-16; Acts 1 [minus Judas]). In other places the same event is repeated in the course of Acts' narrative: the account of Paul's conversion in Acts 9 is repeated not once, but twice (see Acts 22 and 26). Likewise, the encounter between Peter and Cornelius (Acts 10) is repeated in Acts 11, and the contents of the apostolic decree of Acts 15 are repeated in Acts 21.

The Third Gospel, on the other hand, shows an inclination to avoid parallel scenes. Henry Cadbury commented that

> the Gospel, if we may assume that it used Mark, not only omits the second of Mark's accounts of feeding the multitude, but appears to cancel his account of Jesus in his home town (Mark 6:1-6), and of his anointing by a woman (Mark 14:3-9), and perhaps other sayings or scenes in Mark by introducing, before he comes to these scenes, independent versions (Luke 4:16-30; 7:36-50, etc.). Matthew on the contrary appears to repeat passages from Mark a second time.[129]

Such contrast in narrative technique questions whether the implied author of Acts is so easily to be identified with the implied author of Luke.[130]

PROBLEMS IN DESCRIBING THE LUKAN NARRATION

Several objections could be lodged against the above analysis. There is both the problem of sources in Luke and Acts and the

---

[129] Ibid., 89. We should note that a similar comment could be made if one followed the two-gospel theory and assumed that Luke made use of Matthew. For further examples of Luke's avoidance of repetition (using the two-source theory), see Henry J. Cadbury, *Style and Literary Method*, 83–89.

[130] The implied author is also responsible for the "norms of the narrative" or what Chatman (*Story and Discourse*, 149) calls the "general cultural codes." Given the increasing interest in the social world of the biblical narratives, it would be interesting for someone to conduct a study on the social location(s) of Luke and Acts, similar to the one produced by Vernon Robbins without assuming the unity of those two writings (see "The Social Location of the Implied Author of Luke-Acts").

question of discontinuity not only between Luke and Acts but within each narrative. These objections will be addressed in turn.

The Problem of Sources

These distinctions could be explained in part by Lukas's use of sources in Luke and Acts. After all, Jesus speaks in parables because Lukas's source(s) recorded Jesus as speaking in parables. Likewise, the narrator of Acts depicts the disciples as giving long speeches because his sources so presented the disciples. To what extent, then, are some of the differences (e.g., the extent of participation in the story, etc.) controlled by the story line? Certainly, the author's sources limited his choices in the showing and telling of his story.

This fact separates historical writings — even historical "novels" — from pure fiction,[131] but the use of sources still does not adequately resolve the differences which exist at the level of narrative discourse in Luke and Acts. At the conclusion of his analysis of Lukan style, Nigel Turner commented: "One thing is certain, whatever his sources may have been, and however extensive, . . . the final editor has been able to impose his own style upon all his material."[132] One solution is that the two narratives have different narrators, that is, they tell their story differently.

Discontinuity within Luke and Acts

Form and source critics have long noted the changes in styles within the narratives of Luke (especially between chapters 1–2 and 3–24) and Acts (between chapters 1–12 and 13–28). Their proposed solutions were to suggest interpolations or the use

---

[131] Even ancient romantic novels were often based upon a story or source, and free invention of narrative plots was not a normal license in antiquity.

[132] Nigel Turner, *Style*, 57.

of different sources.[133] But J. Hawkins has demonstrated that at least in terms of vocabulary, there are few places where appreciable differences can be noted between Acts 1–12 and 13–28.[134]

The important question of whether each individual Gospel is a unified narrative has only recently come to the forefront in studies by narrative critics. Stephen Moore notes that the discontinuities which source critics identified represent gaps and fissures from a narratological point of view.[135] Scholars, reacting against their own history of fragmenting, have attempted to recover the "wholeness" and integrity of the text. This emphasis on the unity of the text has made it difficult to appreciate the significance such narrative gaps have in literary strategies. As Rimmon-Kenan has observed:

> How to make a bagel? First you take a hole. . . . And how to make a narrative text? In exactly the same way. Holes or gaps are so central in narrative fiction because the materials the text provides for the reconstruction of a world (or a story) are insufficient for saturation. No matter how detailed the presentation is, further questions can always be asked; gaps always remain open.[136]

These observations raise several questions about the foregoing analysis. If Luke and Acts form one narrative at the discourse level, and if gaps are inherent to a narrative, then would not one expect to find just such discontinuities between Luke and Acts? Further, if one compared the discourse level of Luke 1–2 with that of 3–24, or Acts 1–12 with 13–28, could not one establish "distinct" narrative voices, even different narrators,

[133] Hans Conzelmann (*The Theology of Luke*) rejected Luke 1–2 as being integral to the narrative; see the rebuttal by Paul Minear, "Luke's Use of the Birth Stories," 111–130; Raymond E. Brown, *The Birth of the Messiah*, 241–243. C. C. Torrey (*Composition and Date of Acts*) distinguished I Acts (1–15) which had a written Aramaic source underlying the first fifteen chapters and was translated by Luke; and II Acts (16–28) which showed no evidence for an underlying Semitic document. Torrey's thesis received mixed responses. See especially the extensive reviews by Henry J. Cadbury, "Luke—Translator?" 436–455; E. J. Goodspeed, "The Origin of Acts," 83–101.

[134] A conclusion also reached by Levinsohn, *Textual Connections*.

[135] Stephen Moore, "Are the Gospels Unified Narratives?" 443–458.

[136] Rimmon-Kenan, *Narrative Fiction*, 127.

within the same narrative? In other words, how does establishing narration distinct in Luke from Acts demonstrate discontinuity on the discourse level? These are important questions that must be addressed.

The response is two-fold. First, the discontinuities between Luke and Acts are qualitatively different from those within each narrative. The literary techniques distinguished in Luke and Acts, like the textual connectors, the framing devices, first-person narration, are significant in establishing disunity at the discourse level.

Further, Luke and Acts deal with real texts preserved in a manuscript tradition with identifiable beginnings, middles, and endings. The end of both Luke and Acts is followed by an expanse of white space. A narrative composed of Luke and Acts remains a scholarly hypothesis. And even if the two works were intended to form one narrative, most likely early readers read them separately because of publication limitations.[137] The gap between Luke 24 and Acts 1 [in the canon, that "gap" is the Fourth Gospel!] is greater than any crack within either narrative.

CONCLUSION

Scholars have proposed various solutions to the problematical relationship between Luke and Acts. Some have argued that the same author wrote both documents at the same time, producing a two-volume work that from its inception was conceived as "one continuous narrative." Others, perhaps the majority, attempted to account for both the similarities and differences in style by arguing that the same author wrote both documents but at different times and in response to different issues. A few scholars have argued that the documents were produced by different authors at different times, with the similarities due to the conscious efforts of one

---

[137] The problem of composition and publication was discussed in chapter 2.

author to imitate the other and thus legitimate his own writing with the proper requisite authority.

The time has now come to reevaluate the relationship between these two documents using the most recent tools available. This chapter has attempted to do that from a literary perspective and has concluded that, at least on the discourse level, there are significant differences between Luke and Acts.

Though the preceding investigation has been less than exhaustive, it has, at least, shown the need for detailed analysis using the most recent methods available to reassess the unity of Luke and Acts at the discourse level. The conclusion to which this preliminary study leads is that at the discourse level it is inappropriate to speak of the narrative unity of Luke and Acts. These two works are independent narratives with distinct narration, that is, they each tell the story *differently*. That there is some kind of interrelationship between the Lukan writings is evident from the opening line of Acts. And one can make a good case that Acts is the best commentary on Luke (and vice versa) along the lines that prompted Bultmann to suggest that the Johannine Epistles were the best commentary on the Fourth Gospel. But Bultmann's comment did not lead to the conclusion that the epistles were intricately entwined into John, or even that they were written by the same person. So it is for Luke and Acts. In the words of Allen Walworth: "Both volumes are addressed to Theophilus, but different books by the same author to the same reader may easily expect different reader 'moves.' In other words, even if it is the same author and reader who dance together in both Luke and Acts, they do not have to dance in both to the same music."[138]

If Luke and Acts tell the story *differently*, do they tell *different* stories? Or, can the narrative, in Chatman's categories, be distinct at the *discourse* level and an essential unity at the *story* level? Barbara Herrnstein Smith has forcefully criticized Chatman's two-tiered approach to narrative as a kind of platonic idealism. In a nutshell, she views the abstract story level as unworkable

---

[138] Walworth, "Narrator in Acts," 11.

and argues that if the same story is told in different versions at the discourse level, one might argue that the result is two different stories, not two versions of the same story.[139] These comments raise serious questions about the kind of unity which Robert Tannehill, for example, finds in Luke and Acts. The narrative unity about which he writes is almost exclusively at the level of story and does not reckon adequately with the disunity at the discourse level.[140] And if it is possible that this story level exists only in the construal of the modern reader, then the assumption of narrative unity between Luke and Acts needs serious reexamination. Whether the relationship of Luke and Acts deserves the label two-volumed work, or single volume with sequel, or something else can only be determined by examining the various aspects of unity suggested in this volume; it can no longer be an a priori assumption.

[139] Barbara Herrnstein Smith, "Narrative Versions, Narrative Theories," 213–236. Smith does allow for the fact that some types of narratives (historical reports, gospels, twice-told tales) "are the accounts of events that have presumably already occurred in some determinate chronological sequence," and therefore "it makes sense to speak of the narrative . . . as having rearranged the sequence of some given set of events or the events of some given story" (228). Thus, one could argue that the narrative does exist at both the story and discourse levels. This point is important in discussions about whether or not the Four Gospels are four versions of one story or simply four different stories, but it does not vitiate the problem of speaking of the unity of Luke and Acts at the discourse level.

[140] In fact, Tannehill's entire two-volume commentary is focused almost exclusively on the story level, the meta-narrative which Tannehill constructs as part of his retelling of Luke and Acts.

4

The Theological Unity of Luke and Acts

The study of Lukan theology is essentially a product of redaction criticism. This and the central place still held by the pioneering work of H. Conzelmann[1] have established the Gospel of Luke as the main battleground.[2] Until recently analysis of Lukan theology has tended to lag behind the understanding of Luke and Acts as a unity.[3] Theological studies of Acts have, by and large, given priority to the speeches. The grounds for this reflect the presuppositions of redaction criticism; the speeches are generally seen as Lukan compositions and thus give secure access to the author's own ideas. This procedure lends only limited support to the view of Luke and Acts as a unity, for it appears to focus only on the most noteworthy difference between the two books.

The contrast lessens with the realization that theological

---

[1] This monograph was appropriately, if colorlessly, entitled *The Theology of St. Luke* in translation. Earlier scholars did, of course, take note of many Lukan theological interests and themes, but did not attempt to characterize them as a theology proper. Conzelmann's views may, despite sharp criticism, still be described as central in that nearly every study of Lukan theology begins with efforts to support, modify, or refute them.

[2] Conzelmann's study focused, as critics noted, almost exclusively on Luke. His subsequent commentary on Acts was an implicit response to this charge. *The Acts of the Apostles* reaffirms Conzelmann's theories and contains many apposite and incisive theological observations, particularly upon the speeches.

[3] Many articles and a small number of books have been devoted to theological issues in Acts. By and large these give the Gospel only limited attention. O'Toole's work represents the contemporary approach.

analysis of the Gospel has also given particular scrutiny to discourse material. Conzelmann's description of Lukas's re-writing of Mark 13 constitutes one of his most persuasive arguments.[4] His critics, for their part, have often appealed to other speeches.[5] Debates over sources, editing, and the requisite extent of consistency dominated a quarter-century of research.

If questions about the use or non-use of Mark and Q have made analysis of the gospel speeches difficult at points, there are also problems in constructing Lukan theology *via* a précis of the speeches of Acts. In the first place, Lukas does not simply borrow from missionary and other sermons of his own day. The "primitive" elements of the speeches in Acts 1–4 may well be a literary device to evoke the aura of the early days.[6]

In the second place, the speeches are often appropriate to their narrative contexts.[7] This observation should not only caution against generalizations from individual addresses[8] but also raise the question of narrative context. The speeches belong to the narrative and must be analyzed in this context rather than as detachable entities. R. Tannehill has made the most sustained effort to date to present such an analysis.[9] Yet it is questionable whether his (or other) narrative studies have produced, or even attempted to produce, a comprehensive Lukan theology, despite their penetrating exposition of theological and other themes.[10]

Some may regard any attempt to derive abstract ideologies from narratives as a misplaced enterprise from the outset, but

---

[4] See Conzelmann, *Theology*, 125–132, on Luke 21:5-36.

[5] Conzelmann's critics point in particular to the speeches in Luke 12:1-59 and 17:20-37. Another resource for Lukan particular material is the central section (9:51—19:44). See the works of Donahue, Drury, and Moessner, et al.

[6] O'Toole, *Unity*, 154; Plümacher, "Historiker," 254.

[7] This is most apparent in the Areopagus Address of Acts 17:22-31.

[8] Consistent application of the criterion of narrative suitability will avoid *ad hoc* appeals to disregard an intractable element in a particular speech by reference to the narrative setting.

[9] *Narrative Unity*, vol. 2.

[10] Tannehill treats, for example, the question of the place of the Jews within Lukan salvation history in great detail while remaining faithful to his narrative program and seeks to correlate his findings on this question with other data, but does not attempt to integrate this into a systematic theological scheme.

when dealing with partisan religious texts presented by a reliable and omniscient narrator, it is possible to discover at least some features of that narrator's theology. In the specific case of Luke and Acts, the result of such investigations may conveniently be characterized as Lukan theology.

The priority usually given to Luke in studies of Lukan theology is questionable on redaction-critical (and other) grounds. Every problem relating to the unities of Luke and Acts derives from the basic question: Why did Lukas deem it desirable to write a second volume? This prominent issue should not exclude another question: Why did Lukas consider it desirable to compose the *first* volume? Gospels alone are well attested, as are Acts alone.[11] The Lukan combination is unique among surviving texts.[12]

The existence of the two volumes is evidence that the problem of the theological unity of Luke and Acts is first and foremost the problem of continuity, of the relation of the life and activity of the Church to the "Christ-event."[13] In Bultmann's classic formulation, the two volumes of Lukas seek to deal with the tension between proclaimer and proclaimed.[14] Efforts to find the central

[11] The relation between canonical and apocryphal Acts is a matter of some debate, but there are sufficient similarities to allow this question to be posed. Among both the various Gospels and several Acts there are substantial differences yet these allow for general comparison. One cannot resolve the matter by asserting that the canonical Acts follow many apostles, the apocryphal only one, for this is not correct on either account. See Pervo, *Profit.*

[12] The pseudepigraphic endings to Mark, in particular Mark 16:9-20, reflect a (presumably) second-century approval of this means of bridging the gap between Easter and the church. The ultimate common canonical arrangement permits Acts to perform for all four Gospels the role that "longer ending" plays for Mark. In literary terms this is the problem of the "sense of an ending." Mark 16:9-20 and John 21 attest both theological and literary needs to be met.

[13] In broad salvation-historical terms the issue is the relation of Christian faith to the faith of Israel. From the perspective of Christian history the issue is the legitimacy of the Pauline missionary heritage. Lukas characteristically seeks to address these questions by narration rather than by argumentation.

[14] *Theology*, 1:33-37. Bultmann pointed to the tension between the "Synoptic Jesus" as subject of proclamation about God's reign and Pauline theology, in which the heavenly Christ is the object of proclamation. Acts has relatively little to say about the earthly life of Jesus. In Acts the proclaimers of the proclaimed also identify with the life of the proclaimer, but, whereas Paul

unity of Lukan theology are, in the last analysis, evaluations of how successfully Lukas solved this dilemma.

The resurrection marks and establishes a great divide, presented in the narrative as a transformation in theological understanding by Jesus' followers. They, at least, have a different theology in the second volume. Can the narrator show and tell these changes without himself altering his theology or revealing theological concepts held in abeyance in the first volume? If the narrator of Luke must resort to the stratagem of veiling his theology in small or large part, then the theology of Luke is, in that degree, a fictional creation of the narrator.

Since Acts represents most emphatically the particularity of Lukas's contribution and is, presumably, the volume in which the narrator enjoyed greater freedom,[15] there are strong grounds for the working hypothesis that Acts will reveal Lukan theology in its full-fledged form. Nonetheless, this hypothesis languishes in desuetude. Had it routinely been followed, it is difficult to imagine that debate over such subjects as eschatology and the meaning of Jesus' death would have followed the paths that they have so clearly marked in scholarship.

The missionary speeches of Acts do not stress the death of Jesus as a saving event. Rather they support the controverted claim that for Lukas this was a martyrdom that seemed to destroy hopes until overcome by the resurrection.[16] The deaths of the

---

stresses identification with the suffering one, Acts portrays the continuity of mighty words and deeds. Lukas, like Paul (to whom he is apparently indebted), addresses the issue by generally substituting "Spirit" for "Kingdom." Nonetheless, "Kingdom" is more prominent in the Gospel, "Spirit" in Acts.

[15] It is tempting to regard Acts as later and thus more mature than Luke, but such hypotheses can be dangerous and are best avoided. The assumption that Lukas began with Luke 1:1 and wrote to Acts 28:31 is undesirable. Luke 1–2, for example, may have been composed later than Luke 3–24. See also chapter 3, above.

[16] The travelers to Emmaus offer this interpretation, Luke 24:20-21. The rejoinder of v. 26 states that the Messiah had to suffer and then enter into glory. The text is (intentionally?) vague enough to permit quite diverse readings. Jesus' death is presented in the antithesis "you killed but God raised" in Acts 2:23-24; 3:15; 4:10; 7:52 (with an interesting narrative context: the death of Stephen), 10:39-40; 13:29-30. Acts 17:3 closely parallels Luke 24:26. 17:31 refers to the

prophets, Jesus, Stephen, and the "Passion" of Paul[17] belong to an ancient pattern, the repetition of which does little to place Jesus' own death in a unique light.[18] For Lukas the new information of the gospel is not that the Messiah will redeem by dying but that the Messiah must suffer like a prophet before entering into glory.[19]

The centrality of eschatology in debates about Lukan theology also derives from focus upon the Gospel, which allows at least a foothold for those who argue for imminence and more ample ground for the partisans of a "delayed parousia." In Acts, however, eschatology is not a pervasive concern, for references to the end all but disappear after the first four chapters.[20] Of imminence there is nothing of explicit character.[21] When the narrator casts an eye to the future it is false teachers who appear on the horizon, not the parousia.[22]

Similar observations could be made about the present and future dimensions of salvation.[23] If salvation is often portrayed as a present and immediate reality in the Gospel, Acts may be

---

resurrection alone, setting the theme for the remainder of Acts. Chapter 22 refers to the Risen One, and the hope or promise of resurrection dominates the remainder (cf. 23:6; 24:15; 25:19; 26:6-7; 28:20). According to Acts 26:23 Jesus, as first raised from the dead, becomes the basis of the proclamation of light. Luke and Acts proclaim Jesus' victory over death as the harbinger and cause of salvation, rather than the death itself. See J. Tyson, *Death of Jesus.*

[17] Neyrey (*Passion*) is one of many scholars to note the parallels between Jesus' passion in Luke and Paul's progress toward Jerusalem (and Rome) in Acts.

[18] One can argue that the death of Stephen, for example, has a soteriological quality. Cf. O'Toole, *Unity,* 67.

[19] Luke and Acts relate the present of salvation to Jesus' birth (Luke 2:11), ministry of healing (Luke 5:26; cf. 13:32), proclamation (Luke 4:21; 19:5-9), and exaltation (Acts 13:33). With this the "today" of the crucified Jesus (Luke 23:43) is continuous, identical to the announcement to Zacchaeus in Luke 19:5-9.

[20] Acts 17:31 speaks of a judgment, but without eschatological coloring. In Acts the stress is usually upon the resurrection of just and unjust alike. On this matter, see Gaventa, "Peril," 20–22.

[21] Acts 3:20 may seem to suggest imminence, but note the following v. 21. In any case Acts 1:6-7 set the tone for the work. See O'Toole, *Unity,* 152.

[22] Acts 20:17-38. esp. 29-30. Unlike Jesus in Luke 21, Paul does not in his farewell address, utilize the end as a basis for warning and consolation. Contrast Luke 21:34-36 with Acts 20:28-38.

[23] See the survey in Bovon, *Luke,* 239–289.

used to make a case for its essential futurity. Integration of the Christology (-ies) of Luke and Acts presents additional challenges, challenges that initially appear insuperable. Since the Enlightenment scholars have dealt with the impact of post-resurrection Christology upon the "life of Jesus" portrayed in the Gospels. By reporting both pre- and post-exultation experiences of Jesus' followers, the narrators of Luke and Acts permit investigation of this question.

This brief review[24] leads to the observations that the theological unity of Luke and Acts is not a foregone conclusion and that the priority of Luke or Acts (or neither) is a crucial component of the discussion. The investigation will not benefit from the presumption that it will yield a thorough and consistent Lukan theology. If at one time scholars assumed that Lukas had no real theology, contemporary research may expect more consistency than an early Christian author of popular narrative was prepared to supply.[25]

Despite the general moves in scholarship beyond redaction criticism, the call for study of Luke and Acts as a unity, and the emergence of narrative criticism, Lukan theology is still largely engaged in questions raised and shaped by these earlier approaches. Deeming it desirable to launch a probe of Lukan theology that gives due weight to Acts as well as Luke, narrative no less than discourse, and wishing to find another mode for addressing some of the issues in dispute, this exploration will pursue an understanding of Lukan anthropology. Anthropology is no doubt a more subtle and possibly a less intentional

---

[24] These observations do not exhaust the topics about which questions of unity may be raised. Others include social ethics (on which see chap. 2). The almost wholesale critique by recent American scholars of Conzelmann's and Haenchen's view that Lukan thought is colored by a "Theology of Glory" rests in large part upon Luke, although Tannehill (*Narrative Unity*, vol. 2) attempts to find support for the position from Acts.

[25] On consistency in Lukan theology, see Pervo, review of J. Fitzmyer, *The Gospel according to Luke I-IX, ATR* 66 (1984):443–445. For Lukas as a popular writer and theologian, see Pervo, *Profit*. Moreover, ancient religious texts often fail to meet present day standards of consistency, and strict consistency is unlikely for the experimental efforts of a relatively new religion.

component of Lukan theology than salvation history, but it is, as we shall attempt to show, an important and pervasive element of Lukan thought and literary expression that stresses general cultural views rather than particular concerns emerging from the Israelite religious tradition. One narrative perspective anthropology will clearly affect is characterization, which provides a point of entry.

CHARACTERIZATION

Ancient popular narratives, including the various acts and romantic novels, have long been the targets of critical attention on the grounds of their rather stereotyped treatment of plot and character.[26] The characters are not unlike those of the good, old-fashioned "B" movie. Episodes revolve around one figure whose experiences move the plot along. The good act from noble motives; wicked people yield to baser impulses. Conflicts are resolved in favor of the former, confirming the readers' desire for fairness in the world. These qualities are due to more than limited imagination, ethical naiveté,[27] popular taste, and even the requirements for salvation-historical schematization. Modern disapproval of them derives from a fundamental misunderstanding of ancient literature.[28]

These popular writings readily compared their heroes to divinities. Just as apostolic missionaries exhibited god-like

[26] In the case of the canonical Acts the normal explanation for this phenomenon proceeds from the Lukan interest in (salvation historical) patterns of parallelism. For the apocryphal acts it has generally sufficed to speak of monotony and a rather low tone. Criticism of ancient romantic novels once paralleled, in the language of esthetic rather than theological disappointment, what church historians have frequently opined about the apocryphal acts.

[27] Ethically, narratives of this sort provide both comfort and stimulation to the moral life, for they imply rewards for proper behavior and portray the life of virtue as full of adventure and romance. To dismiss all such works as "escapist" is inadequate.

[28] See M. A. Tolbert's lucid summary of the difference between "illustrative" and "representative" characters (*Sowing*, 76–77). Ancient literary characters tended to illustrate qualities rather than represent human realities.

characteristics, so the male and female leads of the romantic
novels struck more ordinary mortals as gods striding upon earth.
One needed but to glimpse them to feel the jovian thunder-
bolt of love.

In the first book of *Callirhoe,* for example, the vile pirate
Theron prepares to exhibit the heroine, whom he has kid-
napped, to a prospective purchaser:

> He uncovered Callirhoe's head, shook her hair loose,[29] and then
> opened the door and told her to go in first. Leonas and all the people
> in the room were awestruck at the sudden apparition — some of them
> thought they had seen a goddess, for people did say that Aphrodite
> manifested herself in the fields.[30]

Apostles, as a famous example will presently illustrate, had
similar experiences. Why? Is this simply a literary convention
in novels and a theological point in the acts?[31] Or does there
hover behind such scenes a kind of anthropological understanding? Investigation of the latter option opens the way to
find in the ancient novels a clue to the popularity of such concepts. Hans Conzelmann, to whose astute identification of
theological issues scholars will long remain indebted, observed
that Lukas had no theoretical anthropology and thus no aware-
ness of the problem of miracle.[32]

Although it is doubtless correct that Lukan theology is
popular, frequently enough insufficiently reflective, and occa-

[29] Cf. 1 Cor. 11:2-16.

[30] Chariton, *Chaereas and Callirhoe,* 1,14, trans. B. P. Reardon, *Collected Ancient Greek Novels,* 36. This is the earliest fully-extant example of the Greek romance. Examples could be multiplied. *Callirhoe* opens with the statement that her beauty was not human (ἀνθρώπινον) but divine (θεῖον), 1.1,2. Other references include Xen. Eph., 1.2,5, Hel. 1,2.5, 2.2,1–2, and Longus 4.33.4. *JosAs* 5–6, discussed in n. 113 below, is an important presentation of this theme in a Jewish context. On the topic see B. Egger, "Women," 50–61; C. Burchard, "Joseph and Aseneth," in *The Old Testament Pseudepigrapha,* vol. 2, p. 191, and Pervo, *Profit,* 134–135.

[31] Nock states that this is no more than a literary convention in the roman-tic novels (*Essays* 1:171).

[32] The problem of miracle for Lukas differed from the problem as conceived by Conzelmann. In addition to the discussion in this chapter, see S. Garrett, *Demise.*

sionally inconsistent, this does not mean that no theoretical basis for Lukan anthropology existed. Here, as often, the lack of agreement between Lukas and Paul has apparently colored the issue. Even if Lukas were aware, directly or indirectly, of Pauline anthropology, he did not accept it. Before denouncing this as a treacherous deviation from Paul and/or the lack of specific development, it is desirable to reflect upon the nature and implications of sin, miracle, and anthropology in Luke and Acts.

A Lukan Parallel

After Paul and Barnabas had healed a cripple at Lystra (Acts 14:6-18) the effervescent local "barbarians," who, moreover, have a famous blot on their copybook, overreact and greet the missionaries as gods. A fine little speech caps an amusing scene. Profit with delight.

Examination of the former is profitable. The Lystrans claim, "The gods have come down to us in human form" (ὁμοιωθέντες ἀνθρώποις; Acts 14:11). The implicit rationale for this assertion is their understanding of the healing as an epiphany: working such a wonder requires a god, and polymorphy is a divine prerogative that mortals will ignore at hazard. Paul and Barnabas have an anthropological term of their own, nicely parallel: ὁμοιοπαθεῖς (mortals just like you),[33] through which they insist that they share their would-be worshipers' condition and nature. They do not make this claim in order to prove that they could not have worked the healing, but (in part) to insist that such actions do not demand the manifest presence of a god. Their

[33] On the significance of this term, see *Wis* 7:1-10 (esp. v. 3); Ps 143:4 (LXX); Heb 2:17; *4 Macc.* 12:13. Gen 3:5, 22; *Wis* 3:10, 14; 1 John 3:2; and Jas 3:9; 5:17. (The last citation refers to Elijah, ὁμοιοπαθὴς ἡμῖν, who was able to control nature through prayer.) Note also Philo *Vita Mos.* 2.61, which states that the human race would be preserved because of its likeness to God (ἕνεκα τῆς πρὸς αὐτὸν ὁμοιότητος). In general see Michaelis, "Μιμέομαι," 5:938–939. Wildhaber (*Paganisme*, 92) underlines the importance of the two *homoi*- (like) statements.

brief oration[34] is notable for its "natural theology."[35]

What is the function of such theology here? It is to argue, in effect, that incidents like the recent healing are but the tip of the iceberg, that the existence of crops and seasons are themselves miracles seen every day and callously overlooked.[36] The healing thus summons the onlookers to observe the miraculous all about them and to confess the God proclaimed by nature.[37]

[34] Vv. 15-17: "Friends, why are you doing this? We are mortals just like you, and we bring you good news, that you should turn from these worthless things to the living God, who made the heaven and the earth and the sea and all that is in them. In past generations he allowed all the nations to follow their own ways; yet he has not left himself without a witness in doing good—giving you rains from heaven and fruitful seasons, and filling you with food and your hearts with joy."

[35] Philo (*Dec.* 178) also speaks of God's maintenance of the universe, including lavish and abundant supply of good to all people at all times and places. See also *Spec. Leg.* 1.168–193, and *Praem.* 9.

In Luke and Acts the theology of creation is also more or less the basis for the abrogation of dietary regulations (cf. Luke 11:40, Acts 10:9-16, Acts 15:20), and thus serves as the basis for the unity of Jews and Gentiles, just as it constitutes the basis for a gentile mission. Aristeas (129) states the problem for traditional observance in the light of this "liberal theology": if the universe is one, how can some foods be unclean?

[36] Appeal to the providential supply of food is frequently the basis for urging mortals to imitate this benefaction. Aristeas 190 (cf. 210 and 259) typifies this mode of exhortation. Note also Philo, *De Abrh* 61: "For anyone who contemplates the order in nature (τήν ἐν τῇ φύσει τάξιν) and the constitution enjoyed by the world-city whose excellence no words can describe, needs no speaker to teach him to practice a law-abiding and peaceful life and to aim at assimilating (ἐξομοίωσιν) himself to its beauties." (trans. F. H. Colson. *Philo*. LCL 6:35)

Acts 14 lacks an explicit ethical thrust. Luke 6:35-36 (n. 71, below), on the other hand, makes the ethical application.

[37] Philo (*Moses* 1.219–224) gives the fundamental perspective. After discussing the water from the rock (Exod 17:1-7; Num 20:1-13), for which he allows natural explanations, Philo proceeds to lambast those skeptics who do not realize that for God wonders are mere child's play. He then invites contemplation of real marvels: stars, sun and moon, seasons, waters, and concludes: "But these things, though truly marvellous, are held in little account because they are familiar. Not so with the unfamiliar: though they be but small matters, we give way before what appears so strange, and drawn by their novelty, regard them with amazement." (trans. F. H. Colson. *Philo*. LCL, 6:387)

The *Sibylline Oracles* reflect the inverse of this popular religious tradition in their appeal to such ominous phenomena as earthquakes (4.128; 5.290-291), flood (4.129, 143-144), and volcanoes (4.130-134) as revelations of divine wrath.

The incident at Lystra does not oppose the realms of nature and grace, the miraculous and the natural; for Luke, like many ancient apologists for miracles, sees nature and miracle as continuous.[38] Salvation history is not the only realm of continuity in Lukan theology. The two words beginning with *homoi-* also indicate a relationship — in this case a relationship between the human and the divine. If the healing stands at the tip of God's gracious creation, the healers represent the zenith of human achievement.

SCIENCE AND MIRACLE IN GRECO-ROMAN ANTIQUITY

The view that miracle conflicts with scientific understanding because of possible "violations of the laws of nature" did not fully emerge until the eighteenth century.[39] There was no educated consensus about scientific laws in the ancient world. Skeptics abounded, of course, but scientific theories, insofar as they existed, were linked to the particular philosophical schools. The debates about divination reveal the absence of agreement.[40] Apologists for particular miraculous accounts or traditions offer scientific justification for the events under review:[41] miracles

[38] As the later theological principle has it: *Gratia non tollit naturam sed perficit* (Grace perfects, not abolishes, nature). Dio of Prusa's *Oration* 12 is a most important contemporary philosophical presentation of the thesis that creation is filled with miracles. Note especially sec. 34, which reads in part: ἀλλ' ἐν τῷδε τῷ κόσμῳ, ποικίλῳ καὶ σοφῷ δημιουργήματι, μυρίων ἑκάστοτε θαυμαστῶν φαινομένων (now in this universe, a deft and complex piece of crafting, with untold marvels manifest at every moment). See also sec. 58.

[39] R. Grant (*Miracle*, 206) states that the first use of the expression ὑπὲρ τὴν φύσιν (surpassing the limits of nature) is to be found in Origen. For ancient views of nature, see H. Koester, "φύσις," 9:251–277, esp. 260–271 and 276–277.

[40] The extent of discord about divination is apparent from the sources cited in Cicero's *De Divinatione* and the material collected by A. S. Pease in his commentary. The Skeptics (including Academics) and Epicureans rejected divination. Most Stoics found divination supportive of their world-view.

[41] Sources in the Lukan milieu include *Wis* 16:4, 24; 19:6, 18-21 and related passages. J. P. M. Sweet ("The Theory of Miracles") and D. Winston (*Wisdom of Solomon*, 300, 323–331) explicate Wisdom's rationalization of miracle in scientific terms and provide numerous parallels, particularly from Philo. (*Creatio ex nihilo* does not form the basis for these arguments.)

did not challenge the structure of the universe; they displayed it.[42] When Luke 23:44, for example, reports the solar failure during the crucifixion of Jesus as an eclipse, this may be called a rationalization of Mark 15:33, but the observation should not lead to the inference that Lukas does not wish the action ascribed to divine Providence.

Excursus 1:
Ancient and Modern Views of the Universe

Since the time of the Industrial Revolution onward power has been construed largely as the capacity to manipulate nature. From this perspective miracle can appear to be an impediment to social progress. One New Testament word for "miracle" (δύναμις) also means "power." Social and political implications were not lacking in antiquity, as stories portraying miracles in conflict situations (such as Mark 2:1-12) indicate, but the categories were quite different from modern ones. Ancients were more likely to envision the universe as a power structure than as a physical structure.

The changed view of the universe that emerged in the Eighteenth Century also challenged the traditional understanding of providence. Both Newton and Leibniz, for example, pictured God as a clock maker. From the newtonian perspective the universe is a watch needing continual maintenance, i.e., divine government and supervision. For Leibniz this attributed

---

B. S. Mackay states that Plutarch "has no conception of a god who had made laws that shall never be broken for the guidance of the universe, and who then, from time to time, steps in and breaks them" ("Plutarch and the Miraculous," 98). Robert Grant observes that "Greek and Roman ideas of nature and the order of nature were subjective and fluid . . . and seemed more rational than they actually were" (*Miracle,* 268).

[42] Modern readers who use the "violation of laws of nature" criterion to define miracle will misunderstand much ancient literature. Does Lukas regard the rescue from shipwreck (Acts 27) as "less miraculous" than Paul's survival of a snake bite and the healing of the sick on Malta (Acts 28:1-10)? Not according to the argument of Acts 14.

imperfection to God, who must have foreseen all. The mechanistic picture of the universe thus raised potential conflicts with traditional notions of providence. This was not true in antiquity. The Aristotelian world view, for example, with its emphasis upon final causes, left room for such concepts as providence. The Stoa pictured the cosmos as an organism, rather than a machine. From this perspective it is not illogical that *1 Clement* 24 makes use of an argument for the orderly course of nature (rather than the unpredictability of grace) to prove resurrection.

THE UNITY OF THE HUMAN RACE

The Lystra tale implies a related theme: human unity.[43] Many voices, Hellenic and other, had been raised against the traditional antithesis between Greeks and barbarians, advocated by no less a worthy than Aristotle.[44] Monarchs pursuing a course of hellenization were likely to find such anthropological dualism an obstacle. It is symptomatic that the leading political symbol of its repudiation was Alexander the Great, who, in this matter,

[43] For general studies of this concept in Greek thought, see A. W. H. Adkins, *From the Many;* and Baldry, *The Unity of Mankind,* together with their references.

[44] Aristotle's *Politics* 1252b is often cited as an example of his contempt for barbarians. See, however, *Nich. Eth.* 1155a, 16–22, for a statement of human unity. The poetic tradition had long before affirmed the unity of humankind, and the Sophists regarded chauvinism as a matter of convention (νόμος) rather than nature (φύσις). The following view is attributed to the Sophist Antiphon:
> We revere and honour those born from noble houses, but those who are not, we neither revere nor honour. In this we behave in a barbarian manner, since we are by φύσις [nature] all born (φῦναι) the same in every respect, both Greeks and barbarians. One may consider the requirements of φύσις, which are compulsory for all humankind ... and in none of these matters is any one of us separated off as barbarian or Greek. We all breathe into the air through mouth and nostrils [cf. Acts 17:25]. (Fr. B44 Diehls-Kranz, excerpts from the translation of Adkins, *From the Many,* 114–116.)

Polybius is the first extant historian to construct a history upon the principle of human unity.

at least, was alleged to have ignored the views of his mentor.[45] The Stoa did much to popularize the notion of a single world and single human race under one god,[46] and through the kind of theology represented by "Euhemerism"[47] such modern and liberal religious views could be coordinated with the ruler-cult, one function of which was the creation of unity and community.[48]

Early Christianity followed trails blazed by diaspora Jews when its representatives took up the program of smashing racial and other barriers with their message of the one God.[49] Lukas thereby presents the Christian mission as an instrument for civilizing barbarians and eliminating barbaric superstition and promoting cultural and racial unity (objects not without attraction to the rulers of the world). Unlike Paul, Lukas does not derive the unity of the human race from the eschatological miracle of new creation through baptism. This unity is an accessible gift of the one God and maker of all, as appears in the more

[45] Alexander's universalism has probably been exaggerated by some modern historians. What is significant here are the views attributed to him by authors of the Hellenistic and Roman periods.

[46] W. S. Kurz justifiably states: "Popular Hellenistic philosophy contained the view that the whole human race is descended from the gods or divine principle" ("Genealogies," 177). For Cynic and other views on the subject, see Baldry, *Unity,* 107–133.

[47] Euhemerus shared a rationalistic view of religious origins that can be traced back to Prodicus, who claimed that humans first worshiped heavenly bodies, subsequently the fruits of the earth, and, ultimately benefactors. In this model the role moderns assign to cultural evolution was played by charismatically endowed individuals, who raised humans from an animal-like condition to civilization. H. Dörrie (*Der Koenigskult*) has posited a direct link between the theological formulations of Euhemerus and the Hellenistic ruler cult. Prodicus's theory is, in effect, the mirror-image of Acts 14:11-17. For the views of Prodicus, see the commentary of A. S. Pease on Cicero, *De Natura Deorum,* 1:260–261, 263; and 2:514–515.

[48] Greco-Roman ruler worship was more than a political device. The conflict between church and empire over this practice and the use of kindred images in christology and imperial theology stem in part from rival efforts to build communities.

[49] See H. D. Betz, *Galatians,* 181–201; and Kurz, "Genealogies," 178. The social function of "one god — one race" in Israelite history could be used by Jews and appropriated by Christians as an argument for universalism, with support from Greek philosophy.

famous of the two speeches on natural theology: The Areopagus address, Acts 17:22-31.[50]

The object cleverly manipulated by Paul as the point of departure for that sermon is the famous inscription "To (an) Unknown God."[51] The audience may be ignorant, but their ignorance is far from invincible.[52] No blindness has utterly corrupted pagan hearts, as Paul presently demonstrates. In due course he comes to the claim that all people descend from one person fashioned by God (v. 26). A scrap of pagan poetry, "We are God's offspring" (v. 28) serves as the text. As in chapter 14, this is linked to an argument from the phenomena of nature, one which now explicitly buttresses the justification of a world mission by claiming common descent from the one God.

Excursus 2:

Human Beings as Offspring of the Divine[53]

The belief that humans are descendants of the gods is a Stoic commonplace,[54] and is related to the stoic view of nature, but the idea found expression from the earliest times. Examples from the Greek tradition include Pindar,[55] Prodicus,[56]

---

[50] In a brief comparison of the Lystra and Areopagus addresses, Dibelius (*Studies,* 71 n. 23) finds the former closer to the LXX in language and form.

[51] Acts 17:23. The narrator apparently adjusted a tradition of dedications to unknown deities to the requirements of monotheism.

[52] The Jews of Jerusalem were also ignorant (albeit on another matter; Acts 3:17, the only other use of the noun "ignorance" in the New Testament). Such ignorance may be overcome by repentance in Luke and Acts. The same view underlies the theology of *Joseph and Aseneth.*

[53] Ancient views on humans as the offspring of a god or gods are summarized by G. Delling ("Gotteskindshaft"); Adkins (*From the Many*); Baldry (*The Unity of Mankind*); and W. Speyer ("Genealogie").

[54] For example, Seneca, *Ep. Mor.* 44:1 "Omnes, si ad originem primam revocantur, a dis sunt" (all persons, if they are traced back to their origin, are descendants of the gods).

[55] *Nemean Odes* 6. 1–5.

[56] As reported in Plato, *Protag.* 337c–d.

Cleanthes,[57] Epictetus,[58] Dio of Prusa,[59] Plutarch,[60] and the *Sentences of Sextus.*[61]

Biblical passages could be introduced in support of the view, including Ps 82:6; Jdt 9:4, 13; and Esth 8:12-13.[62] Judaism often ethicized the concept: the righteous are children of God, a view paralleled in the philosophical tradition. Delling states that "children of God" is remarkably frequent in Hellenistic Judaism.[63] A relevant example in the present context is Philo, *Dec.* 64, which speaks of the kinship of all created things under one father, the fashioner of the universe.[64]

Cicero is no less informative. After positing reason as the common property of gods and mortals and the universe as one commonwealth with both mortals and gods, the speaker proceeds to speak of a blood relationship, or shared ancestral origin (*agnatio . . . vel genus vel stirps . . .*).[65] Recognition of God (cf. Acts 17:22-31) is based upon this relationship. The common possession of virtue leads to the conclusion that between gods and mortals there is a likeness.[66] There follows an argument for providence from the bounties of nature. This passage reflects many of the themes utilized in Acts 14 and 17.

The most relevant of all parallels is, of course, the *Phainomena* of Aratus, 1-9, a passage from which Acts 17:28 apparently quotes.[67]

---

[57] *SVF* 1, 4, 1, 262, 537, 4.

[58] *Diss.* 1.9.1 and 7, etc.

[59] *Or.* 12.27, 29, 39, 43, 47, 61, 75, 77; and *Or.* 30.26.

[60] *De Exil.* 600.

[61] 58, 135, and 60.

[62] See also *Orac. Syb.* 3,726 and *3 Macc.* 6:28. Byrne provides a review of various uses of "children of God" in Israelite texts.

[63] "Gotteskindschaft," 1163.

[64] *Dec.* 41 speaks of nature as the common mother of all. (Philo's ethical orientation appears in *Conf. Ling.* 145.)

[65] Cicero, *Laws* 1.7.23-24.

[66] *Similitudo* (= ὁμοίωσις), Cicero, *Laws* 1.7.25.

[67] The quotation is from v. 5 of the *Phainomena.* Note also *1 Clem.* 20.4, a passage close in time and viewpoint to the Lukan milieu.

This very common anthropology provides a weapon for the denunciation of idolatry:[68] God's progeny dare not imagine that the Deity, their parent, is like (ὁμοίος) metals or minerals. Acts 17:26-28 and 14:11-18, set forth two *continua:* history (both natural and salvific) and the descent of human beings from God, which establishes all humans as first and foremost world citizens, thereby minimizing national origin. Both are aspects of Lukan thought.

Luke 3:23-38 shows that Acts 17:26-28 is not anomalous. The location of this genealogy may seem anticlimactic, but it gains anthropological significance by proximity to the declaration "You are my Son" (Luke 3:22). Those who compare it to Matthew observe that the genealogy in Luke runs in reverse,[69] so to speak, beginning with Joseph and proceeding back, to Abraham, (Matthew's climactic forebear), and then beyond, to Adam — a characteristic bit of Lukan universalism, moving beyond specifically Jewish history to the common ancestor of Jews and Gentiles, Greeks and barbarians, alike. By so extending the genealogy, Lukas has placed his story in a universal context, affirming the essential unity of the human race. This genealogy justifies (and foreshadows) a gentile mission. Through it salvation history and human history coincide.

The genealogy does not, however, end with Adam, but with God: "Adam, offspring of God" (Luke 3:38). This prefigures Acts 17:28 and thwarts any attempt to brush aside the poetic quotation as mere ornamental flourish. Moreover, the climactic "Son of God" forms a dramatic inclusion with Luke 3:22. In what way is Jesus the Son of God? By virtue of adoption at baptism? Not according to Luke. The conception through the Holy Spirit (Luke 1:26-38) cannot be overlooked, but Luke 3 does proclaim

---

[68] In his essay, "The Areopagus Speech," D. Balch provides a recent analysis of this critique of idolatry based upon the revelation of God in nature. See also *Wis* 13:11-9. The belief that nature reveals God also constitutes a basis for the critique of idolatry, as in *Wis* 13:1-9.

[69] Kurz states that the "ascending" form of Jewish genealogy emerges in the Hellenistic period. He notes Ezra 7:1-5 and *Jdt* 8:1 as examples.

Jesus as Son of God also by virtue of descent.[70] This heritage is shared, needless to say, with all humanity. Does Lukas imply that the divine sonship of Adam comes to its potential in Jesus' birth through the agency of the Spirit? Possibly so, for through the Spirit Jesus realizes and achieves this potential, and Acts portrays the bestowal of that same Spirit upon all believers. Through Adam all people have some kind of status as offspring of God.[71]

Lukas presumably refers to Adam not as a fallen sinner but as the glorified, immortal being fashioned by God and placed at the head of creation.[72] This splendid figure is worthy of the epithet "Son of God."[73]

---

[70] See, for example, Schürmann, *Lukasevangelium* 1:201–202; Fitzmyer, *Gospel of Luke* 1:504; and Kurz, "Genealogy," 171. Genealogies derived from God are not characteristic of Jewish sources, according to Nolland (*Luke*, 173). Claims of divine descent were, of course, widespread in the Greco-Roman world.

[71] See Luke 1:32, "He [Jesus] will be called great and will be called the Son of the Most High," with Luke 6:35: "You will be children of the Most High," (not paralleled in Matt.). This promise does not refer to a future eschatological condition but to a state realized through imitation of divine mercy.

Imitation of the God or the gods is the ethical imperative consequent upon the indicate of divine parentage in Greco-Roman popular philosophy and Hellenistic Judaism. On this, see W. Michaelis, "Μιμέομαι,"; and A. Schweizer, "υἱός." R. Williamson (*Jews*, 214) summarizes Philo's views on the imitation of God. Schürmann refers to divine kinship as an eschatological gift in *Jub* 1:24-25; *Pss. Sol.* 17:27, 30; *1 Enoch* 62:11; and *Ass. Mos.* 10:3. Byrne ("Sons," 18–70) surveys a wide range of texts. Lukas evidently sought to integrate the baptismal-eschatological understanding of becoming children of God (as in Gal 3:26-28) with the natural understanding, and did so at the expense of the former. The Lukan perspective expressed in 6:35 is essentially that of *Sir* 4:10 (on which see Byrne, "Sons," 25. Cf. also *Sir* 13:15 and 18:13), and thus shares the more optimistic anthropology of a major stream of the wisdom tradition, from which tradition natural theology also takes its roots.

[72] Luke 20:35-38, with its oft-noted parallels to *4 Macc.* 7:19; 13:17; and 16:24-25 exhibit the place of immortality in Lukan thought. In the present context the most important parallel is probably Acts 17:28: "In him [God] we live. . . ." Cf. Luke 20:38: "For all live in him [God]" (author's trans.). V. 36 states that the righteous are immortal and children of God. The concept of immortality goes hand in hand with belief in divine origin. (The variant μέλλουσι in v. 36 signals the inherent problem.) Compare *Aristeas* 16, δι' ὅν ζῳοποιοῦνται τὰ πάντα καὶ γίνεται with Acts 17:28.

[73] Regarding this understanding of Adam, see Jervell, *Imago Dei*, 100–107; and J. Levinson, *Images of Adam*, index, 255, *svv.* "Anthropology" and "Original

Sin and Spirit

What many Western[74] Christians miss in Luke 3:38 is a reference to Adam's sin, to the great rift necessitating redemption,
to the loss of the divine image and the expulsion from paradise.
Luke 4 does not supply this deficit.[75] Armed with the Spirit Jesus
goes into the wilderness[76] and there bests the tempter three
times. Others will succumb at times, but those who rely upon
the Spirit need not fall. The power of evil in Luke and Acts is
not ultimate, nor is the barrier between earth and heaven
impermeable.

Lukan theology does not include a theory of "Original Sin."
Conzelmann remarks:

> No demonstration of human sinfulness is attempted in any part
> of the preaching. In Acts the idea of sin is found only in connec-
> tion with the declaration of its forgiveness. The idea contains no
> cosmological or speculative elements whatever. The saying in Acts

---

nature of *adam*." Texts include *Sir* 49:16; *2 Enoch* 30–31; *The Testament of Abraham;*
and *The Lives of Adam and Eve* 12–22. Levinson rejects the notion of a uniform
portrait of Adam in early Judaism. He also demonstrates that Philo and
Josephus presented the motif of Adam's original splendor in the language of
Greco-Roman anthropology.

[74] For a summary of Eastern views on this subject, see Tsirpanlis (44–53)
who states that one becomes

> the perfect image of God by discovering His likeness, which is the perfec-
> tion of the nature common to all men. The Greek term ὁμοίωσις [likeness]
> ... means precisely that dynamic progress and growth in divine life and
> implies human freedom. In Greek patristic thought there is no opposition
> between freedom ("likeness") and grace (God's image in man) (45–46).

"Likeness" is used in this context, as elsewhere, in relation to capacity for growth
and change.

[75] Compare in this regard *2 Baruch* 54:18-19, which appeals to natural revelation and states that each human has become his or her own Adam. For Lukas
this view may be too extreme, but neither author speaks of a universal fall,
and both see nature as a revelatory instrument.

[76] Wilderness is an ambiguous concept. It is the location of paradise past
and coming advent, as well as the place of testing and failure. The ambiguity
reveals that failure is not inevitable.

7:60 states the concrete fact of sin. ἁμαρτωλός [sinner] is not a general declaration about the human situation. There are people who do not need repentance and forgiveness (Luke 15:3ff.).[77]

S. Brown expanded this observation by demonstrating how Lukas revised Mark to remove the suggestion that evil has ultimate power. In literary terms this would be described in part as a different characterization of the disciples from that of Mark. According to Brown, Luke does not relate sin to an anthropological principle or cause, but prefers the "morally neutral faculty" of καρδία (heart).[78] The same insight led Conzelmann to state that Lukas had no theoretical anthropology.[79] It is preferable to say that this conviction sheds light upon the nature of Lukan anthropology.

There remains, of course, a role for the Spirit. The Lukan notion of the Spirit is not dualistic, a fact emphasized by appearance in bodily form and through various concrete manifestations, including healings, speaking in foreign tongues, and sharing of possessions.[80] This Spirit extends through creation and redemption, uniting the eras of salvation history.[81] Through the exaltation of Jesus the power of the Spirit becomes universally available. Not in conflict with either Jewish or Greco-Roman culture and tradition, the Spirit would guide both to find the gifts God would bestow upon all. It is available to all of Adam's descendants, the basis for and means whereby one

[77] *Theology,* 227 n. 2 (trans. slightly altered). In Luke and Acts sin is always in the plural, referring to deeds rather than to character. The disputed category of "God-fearers" illustrates this unity. Cornelius and his associates represent those who need not repent. They are acceptable in the sight of God (Acts 10:35). Hellenistic Jewish authors presented diverse (sometimes self-contradictory) opinions of what views and practices made Gentiles acceptable to God.

[78] *Apostasy and Perseverance,* 121. S. Garrett (*Demise*) offers further evidence, although not cast in anthropological terms.

[79] *Acts,* xlvii.

[80] W. Grundmann argues that Lukas regarded the Spirit as a substance, "δύναμαι" 2:300–302. Such a view would conform to the perspective of the major Hellenistic philosophical schools, which were materialistic in orientation.

[81] The Spirit achieves unity through inspiration of the prophets, Jesus, and the apostles, and serves as the source of mighty deeds.

may reclaim the heritage of God's children. Paul, by way of comparison, understands the "today" of salvation christologically, as an invitation to accept Christ's redeeming work. Lukas, on the other hand, views the "today" of salvation anthropologically, as a gift.[82]

Between this anthropological view of salvation and the absence of "original sin" there are obvious links. The Adam of Luke 3:38 and Acts 17:26-28 is, as noted, a glorious figure. In Hellenistic Judaism Luke's view of Adam may well have been the dominant one. It is certainly well attested. Anthropologically this portrait of Adam not only proclaims the unity of the human race but also a divine parent whose offspring can recognize their maker, a parent from whom they are not wholly estranged, even if the inheritance has been squandered in a strange land far away.[83] Luke's theology, unlike Paul's, does not take its departure from the assumption of brokenness. For Lukas continuity is crucial. To admit brokenness would be to lose the whole game.[84]

ADAM AND CHRIST

Does Lukas view Christ as a New Adam? J. Neyrey makes a case for a Christology based upon Jesus as a new (glorious) Adam who reverses the events of the fall.[85] He reads the temptation story (Luke 4:1-13) against the background of Genesis 3 and finds correspondences between the temptation and the agony

[82] On the use of "today" in Luke and Acts, see above, n. 19.

[83] As Conzelmann's reference (n. 77 above) implies, the parable of the Prodigal Son (Luke 15:11-32) portrays the Lukan view of sin in narrative form. The prodigal does not require a messenger to expose his condition nor adoption to reclaim his status. Self-discovery leads to change (15:17). His father did not see their relationship as broken ("dead and alive" are softened by correlation with "lost and found," vv. 20-32). With repentance comes a restoration of the younger son's former life.

[84] Georgi (*Opponents*, 246–250, 252–254, and 278) finds a similar dimension in the theology of Paul's opponents in 2 Corinthians.

[85] *Passion*, 165–174 *et passim*.

The Theological Unity of Luke and Acts

in Gethsemane (Luke 22:39-46).[86] Talbert makes a similar observation with regard to the Lukan genealogy: Jesus, like Adam, is a "direct creation of God."[87] Adam also figures in the Areopagus Address, where both he and Jesus are anonymous.[88] Adam and Jesus have much in common. Both are "Sons of God," but also human beings, for Lukas regards Jesus as truly human, not as preexistent or as endowed with gifts unavailable to other persons.[89] For Adam, Jesus, and every other person temptation can be resisted and the Devil thwarted.[90] The importance of this comparison, then, is not the contrast between a Christ who restored what Adam lost, but in the qualities not lost by Adam that Jesus and others share.

---

[86] Kloppenborg (*Formation*, 246–262) provides a range of interpretation of the Q temptation story. Neyrey does not observe that Luke 22 has no reference to a garden or to Gethsemane, but to the Mt. of Olives (v. 39). For background he refers to *T.Levi* 18:10-12. Neyrey's discussion of "Gethsemane" stresses Jesus' moral victory in an ἀγών (contest) with temptation and contains important insights into Lukan anthropology. Nolland (*Luke*, 1:182) finds in the Temptation a "touch of Adamic typology," but does not see it as central.

[87] *Reading*, 45.

[88] Acts 17:26: "From one ancestor he made all nations to inhabit the whole earth"; v. 31: he has fixed a day on which he will have the world judged in righteousness by a man he has appointed."

[89] Peter, Paul, and others perform similar deeds, as had figures like Moses, Elijah, and Elisha prior to Jesus. Acts 17:31 calls even the glorified Christ a "man." On preexistence in Luke, see R. Brown, *Birth*, 313–314.

[90] Lukas avoids speculation about the image of God, which had already vexed Paul (1 Cor, esp. ch. 15) and later Paulinists (Col and Eph). Gen 1:26-27; 2:7; and 5:1-8 continued to trouble patristic authorities. Lukas adheres to the Genesis tradition by using ποιεῖν (make) as the verb to describe creation (e.g., Luke 11:3; Acts 14:15; 17:21, 26), including the creation of Adam (Acts 17:24). Gen 1:26 uses both "image" and "likeness" (ὁμοίωσις). Lukan anthropology proceeds from the latter. Both terms had been important in the history of thought since Plato, who described the cosmos as the εἰκὼν τοῦ νοητοῦ θεὸς αἰσθητός (a perceptible god, the image of the intelligible; *Timaeus* 92C) and the ethical life as ὁμοίωσις θεῷ πρὸς τὸ δυνατόν (the greatest likeness to god possible; *Theatetus* 176B [on which see J. Schneider, "ὅμοιος," 5:191]). Lukas prefers a moralizing understanding, which appears consonant with *homoi-* terminology, as in James 3:9 (on which see n. 33 above).

105

COMMUNALISM

The utopian-eschatological view of possessions[91] set forth in Luke and Acts reflects a similar program of restoring the (primeval) unity of the human race through sharing. The anthropology underlying this view is that set forth above. In Jewish terms it reflects the restoration of paradise. In pagan terms this life represents achievement of an ancient philosophical goal, one often given literary expression in utopian novels and descriptions of the golden age when humans were not obsessed with sex and greed.[92] In these works the utopian program may include the restoration of primitive religion (possibly based upon religio-historical theories).[93] The Pentecost miracle demonstrates that the role of the Spirit is not to bring about ecstatic manifestations but rather to restore primitive unity.[94]

The anthropological underpinning of this view of possessions, with its ethical implications, are those set forth above. Humanity can achieve the splendors of its original state. Once again, anthropology provides Lukas with a basis for intergrating traditional Jewish and Greco-Roman concepts.

[91] See Pervo, *Profit*, 69–70 and the references there; and, in general, L. T. Johnson, *Literary Function*. The Lukan view of marriage conforms to this ideal. See P. Brown, *Body*, 93, *et passim*.

[92] Ferguson gives a recent survey of ancient utopian thought in general. One interesting example in the present context (see previous note) is Herodotus 4.104, in which communal marriage is the vehicle for making one family of the human race and the consequent elimination of jealousy and strife. Lukas shared these values. The myth of the Golden Age, often linked to the understanding of humans as divine progeny, served as a continual resource for philosophical musings about the ideal society. Both utopian philosophers and eschatological prophets worked with models that presumed future glories would repristinate primitive conditions. Josephus (*Ant* 1.46–51) represents the Garden of Eden as the Greek Golden Age. Prior to the Fall, food was produced of its own volition (αὐτομάτως) through divine providence. Cf. the providential view of the wonders of nature in Acts 14:15-17.

[93] Euhemerus (see above) explicitly develops a religio-historical theory. In this context the speeches of Acts 14 and 17 to gentile audiences are appeals to return to the primitive monotheism of the natural philosophers.

[94] The kindred reactions of the respective audiences in Jerusalem (Acts 2:12-13) and Athens (17:18, 32) reinforce this understanding of the Spirit.

Anthropological Considerations

Behind the preceding sketch stands what is probably the most common (and fluid) of Greco-Roman anthropological perspectives, in which humanity lies upon a spectrum ranging from the θηριῶδες (beastly) to the θεῖον (divine), with a potential for ethical improvement. To return to the original basis of comparison, just as ancient romantic novels were fond of portraying their leading characters' appearances as divine, so were their antagonists often described as savage (and barbaric) beasts.[95]

Plutarch sets humanity between the divine and the beastlike.[96] His gradient is linked to lists of virtues and vices. Belief in moral progress (with its background in the epic tradition) was a firmly-rooted characteristic of such anthropology.[97] Plato had earlier identified three grades: humans, gods, and beasts.[98] H. D. Betz has analyzed this material and provided numerous references.[99] Such a spectrum is implied in Acts 14:6-18, through the view of miracles offered and the prefix *homoi-*, which points in two directions. The Lystrans complete the circle in vv. 19-20 by revealing their beastly aspects.[100]

Aristotle's animate spectrum conveniently ranged from philosophers on the top to animals on the bottom.[101] For his part, Philo places humanity on the boundary between the mortal and the immortal: διὸ καὶ κυρίως ἄν τις εἴποι τὸν ἄνθρωπον θνητῆς καὶ ἀθανάτου φύσεως εἶναι μεθόριον (One may thus quite properly say

---

[95] For example Heliodorus 1.15.5: ᾽Αλλ᾽ ἡ θηριώδης ἐγὼ καὶ ἀνήμερος, 7.24.5; 8.9.10. See Egger, "Women," 82–83. Apuleius develops the theme fully in his *Metamorphoses,* as does the *Acts of Thomas.* Cf. also Ps 72:22 (LXX).

[96] *Moralia* 75–76, *Quomodo Quis Suos in Virtute Sentiat Profectus.*

[97] See also idem, *De Esu Carnis* 996b, which sees divine and demonic forces in opposition. *E apud Delphos* 390E lists in descending order: gods, *daimones,* heroes, humans, animals. Note also, in the same treatise, 416 C–E.

[98] *Rep.* 571d.

[99] "Gottmensch II," 11:236–238.

[100] "Beast" is thus a suitable epithet for one presumed devoid of humanity, including those regarded as tyrants, like Nero (Philostratus, *Life of Apollonius* 4.38; *Syb. Or.* 8.157), or Domitian (Pliny, *Panegyric* 48.3).

that humanity is the boundary land between mortal and immortal nature).[102]

Musonius Rufus states that life according to nature is not the pursuit of pleasure.[103] Beginning with analogies from the animal kingdom, Musonius finds humanity the sole earthly resemblance (μίμημα) to God because of participation in the same (four cardinal) virtues.[104] Contrasted to vices often found in early Christian literature: ἡδονή (desire; Luke 18:14; Tit 3:3), πλεονεξία (greed; Mark 7:22), ἐπιθυμία (lust; Col 3:5), φθόνος (envy; Gal 5:21), and ζηλοτυπία (rivalry; *Didache* 5:1) are the qualities, μεγαλόφρων (noble-mindedness), εὐεργετικός (beneficence), and φιλάνθρωπος (humanitarianism). When humans, the μίμημα of God, live according to nature, they are like God (ὁμοίως ἔχειν; cf. Gen 3:5, 22). The ethical life, characterized as beneficent and philan-thropic, is imitation of God and reflects likeness to God. Closely related is the perspective of Epictetus, *Diss.* 2.14.21–23: the duty of human beings is to strive to be as godlike as possible (κατὰ δύναμιν ἐξομοιοῦσθαι).[105] The adjectives exemplifying such likeness are ἐλεύθερος (free), εὐεργετικός (beneficent), and μεγαλόφορος (noble).

For Lukas, Jesus, in a special and particular but not always distinct way, and the early missionaries are so endowed as to be able to radiate the divine. Their deeds and experiences are the tip of the iceberg revealing the fullness of human poten-tiality. The superhuman is within human grasp.

At the other end of the scale is feral existence, vividly depicted in the parable of the Prodigal Son. Homer viewed mortality as distinguishing humans from gods, and the consumption of bread (i.e., cultivated and prepared food) as marking mortals

---

[101] Baldry, *Unity,* 144.

[102] *De Opificio Mundi* 135. See also *Spec. Leg.* 1.116, which characterizes the High Priest as endowed with a higher nature, employing the same term, and *De Som.* 2.188, which also speaks of the High Priest as hovering between deity and humanity. Lukas's views of Jesus and others are similar to Philo's under-standing of high priestly character.

[103] *Fr.* 17, *What is the Best Viaticum for Old Age?*, Lutz, 106–110.

[104] Lutz, 108.

[105] The reference to Plato, *Theatetus* 176b (cf. n. 90 above), is apparent.

from animals.[106] Later writers were inclined to see reason as the bond between mortals and gods.[107] Ancient anthropologists traced the ascent of the human race from primitive beastliness to civilization through benefits offered by gods or gifted mortals.[108] In Jewish and Christian works wild beasts are often symbols or expressions of the demonic.[109] Exorcisms could be viewed as transformations of Satan's degraded victims into civilized children of God.[110]

By current lights such notions as that of the θεῖος ἀνήρ (divine man) seem to be rather docetic, to present an at least partial denial of true humanity, but this was not the view of antiquity.[111] Lukas is quite as monistic (and "materialistic") as one can be. Such Lukan stories as the transfigurations of Jesus and Stephen

---

[106] Luke 15:11-16, where the prodigal is reduced to lusting for animal fodder, symbolizes the retrogression from human to beast.

[107] For a classic discussion, see Cicero, *De Leg.* 1:22-39. Note also *De Nat. Deorum* 2:79.133.154; Epictetus *Diss.* 1.9.5; Dio of Prusa, *Or.* 36.38; and the references and discussion by Pease in his commentary on the *De Natura Deorum*, 2:895, 951.

[108] The Epicureans painted gripping pictures of primitive beastliness, as in Lucretius, *De Rerum Nat.* 5:783ff., 925ff. Diod. Sic. 3.56 states that Ouranos ended lawlessness (a sign of apocalyptic return to chaos in early Christian writings; cf. Matt 7:23) and feral (θηριώδης) life for the citizens of Atlantis. This is "euhemerism." Earlier Greeks did not hesitate to call "barbarians" animals. For the later shift, see Cicero, *Resp.* 1.58, in which "*inhumanis ac feris*" (inhuman and feral) replaces the customary "barbaric."

[109] The beast (θηρίον) of Revelation is a familiar example. In Daniel beasts supply not only apocalyptic images for the visions of chaps. 7-8, but also serve as instruments of the narrative: the lion's den of chap. 6 and the snake of chap. 14 (LXX). Philosophers applied the epithet to their opponents or to the unphilosophically inclined masses. Tit 1:12 reflects this usage. See Malherbe, *Popular Philosophers*, 14, 21 for references. Opponents are often characterized as "wolves" or "dogs," as in Luke 10:3; Acts 20:29; John 10:12; Matt 7:6; Phil 3:2; and Rev 22:15.

[110] Luke 8:26-39 (cf. Acts 19:13-17) is the outstanding Lukan example of this understanding. Exorcism (Luke 14:1-6) and repentance (Luke 7:36-50) are both means for restoring persons to communal life.

[111] This is not to suggest a uniform and enduring social or ideological type. Despite much valid criticism and refinement, the concept of the "divine person" should not be abandoned, nor should it be restricted to thaumaturges. In antiquity this or a kindred label, applied to widely differing individuals, was a form of praise.

(Luke 9:28-36; Acts 6:15), the veiled Christ on the Emmaus road (Luke 24:13-35), and the disappearances (ἀφάνισμοι) of Jesus and Philip (Luke 24:31; Acts 8:39-40) do not proclaim the absence of human qualities but the realization of latent capabilities.

Metamorphosis supplied the ancients with a flexible tool for exploration of the relations between the one and the many. The Lystrans of Acts 14 assumed that gods could take different forms at will, a view supported by a vast weight of mythological traditions, of which Ovid is only the best-known and most copious source. Lukas does not restrict transfiguration to heavenly beings. Jesus and Stephen manifest their possession of the divine when transfigured while praying.[112]

When the story has a romantic aim, heroes and heroines are taken as manifestations of Aphrodite or Apollo, while the heroes of Luke and Acts are, of course, more notable for their extraordinary wisdom, strength, courage, and rhetorical ability than for their physical beauty,[113] but the similarities are suggestive.

In the terms of modern popular quasi-psychology, Lukan anthropology deals with the totality of human potential, with the prospect of the almost limitless possibilities[114] available to those who claim their divine heritage. Such an anthropology, with its confidence that all people can be righteous and therefore

[112] The face of Stephen is like an angel's (Acts 6:15). Compare the description of the heavenly Adam in *T. Abrh.* 11:4-10, and the just Abel, "a wondrous man, bright as the sun, like unto a son of God" (ἀνὴρ θαυμαστὸς ἡλιόρατος ὅμοιος υἱῷ θεοῦ; 12:5). The use of εἶδος (appearance) in Luke 9:29 does not suggest an eschatological event so much as the revelation of Jesus' true nature.

[113] For a merger of erotic and religious images, see *JosAs,* esp. chaps. 5–6. Asenath laments that she has spurned "the sun from heaven" because she "did not know that Joseph is (a) son of God. For who among men on earth will generate such beauty, and what womb of a woman will give birth to such light?" (6:2-5, trans. C. Burchard, *Joseph and Asenath,* in J. Charlesworth, ed., *The Old Testament Pseudepigrapha,* 177–247, 209) whose notes on this passage and theme should be consulted. In a similar vein, see Josephus, *Ant.* 2:232, which describes the infant Moses as divine in appearance and noble in mind (παῖδα μορφῇ τε θεῖον καὶ φρονήματι γενναῖον); and Acts 7:20-22, which speak of the infant Moses' beauty and his growth to power and wisdom in word and deed.

[114] The final word of Luke and Acts is ἀκωλύτως (unhindered); Acts 28:31.

acceptable to God,[115] is thoroughly optimistic and quite open to moralism. It is thus quite appropriate that the Example Story[116] characterizes the peculiar Lukan contributions to the tradition of Jesus' parables.

S. Stowers adroitly concludes an essay on ancient anthropology with this remark: "Finally, this is the place to remember that constructions of psychology and anthropology are always related to issues of power."[117] Lukas would not disagree. Power is his subject. Its display is his proof. "Spirit and Power" practically constitute a hendiadys (Luke 1:17, 4:14; Acts 10:38). The gospel is framed by promises of power from on high, promises that correlate Christology with anthropology.[118]

The spiritual power Lukas proclaims and offers is both rational and empirical, yet far from in conflict with miracle. Its very description constitutes an invitation to all who saw the pursuit of power as an indispensable adjunct to improving the quality of their lives.[119]

The desire to reach for and achieve the divine potential available to everyone stands behind all of the various Acts, whatever their particular theological orientation, and it is likewise reflected in such works as popular novels. This is one function of stereotyped heroes, after all. Heroism is manifest and definable, admitting little growth and requiring no real

[115] Acts 10:35. Philo depicts such figures as Adam, Noah, and Moses as loyal world citizens, who live in accordance with nature. See *De Opificio Mundi* 3 and 75; *Conf. Ling.* 106; *Vit. Mos* 2:59-65; *Det.* 87.

[116] Example stories include the "parables" of the Good Samaritan, the Prodigal Son, and the Pharisee and the Publican.

[117] "Paul," 286.

[118] Luke 1:35; 24:49. The close correlation of the power that Jesus will receive from the "Most High" (δύναμις; Luke 1:35), and the power promised the apostles in 24:49 (δύναμιν; cf. also Acts 1:7) portrays not only the Lukan understanding of the Spirit but also the Lukan understanding of human potential. Passages like this indicate the degree to which Lukan Christology is an aspect of anthropology.

[119] For further development of this theme, see S. Garret's nuanced discussion of magic in Luke-Acts and its world (*Demise*); and S. Price's discussion of the ruler cult in *Rituals and Power*.

variation.[120] Those who represent achievement of one sort of heroism or another are stereotyped because they are perfect illustrations of attainment. The goals differ: perfect beauty leading to a longed-for love object,[121] union with one's god, adventure galore, *etc.*; and "ideological" frameworks may also differ, but similar views of the human condition and potential underly the various types of writing in question.

For Luke and Acts this means that one should note not only the horizontal salvation-historical continuum of Law-Prophets, Jesus, Church,[122] but also that vertical continuum ranging from the demonic to the divine. Lukas's explication of this anthropology, in which divine origin is the basis for divinely endowed individuals, the presence of whom, in turn, demonstrates that humans are of divine origin, in terms of a Christology produces the theological unity (and disunity) of Luke and Acts. It provided an intellectually acceptable medium for the explication of the succession of prophets and holy leaders. Lukas's challenge was the expression of a distinctive Christology in the light of his anthropology. Since most depictions of a "Theology of Glory" are little more than a polemical parody, those who attribute such a position to Lukas are often presumed to be denigrating Lukan theology.

Denigration of Lukan theology has not been the object of this exploration of Lukan theology from an anthropological perspective. Lukan theology did not lead to escape from, but to engagement with, the world and formed a powerful basis for commu-

---

[120] Popular works usually seek to reinforce basic values and concepts rather than to emphasize ambiguities. Readers are expected to derive reassurance from this confirmation of their world view.

[121] The attractiveness of romantic heroines and heroes does not arise from artifice or wiles; it is a power beyond their disposal and more often brings trouble than pleasure. For a similar view of miraculous healing power, see Luke 8:44-46. (The source is Mark 5:27-31, presumably, but like Matthew, Lukas could have altered this source.)

[122] The model of salvation history is variously construed, but these variations do not affect the immediate argument.

nity edification and organization and the integration of the new cult into imperial society.[123]

CONCLUSION

Lukan anthropology and literary method are thoroughly congruent. The narrator of Luke and Acts found stories of those who exemplify the divine in their lives as the preferred medium for theological expression. From the theological perspective here proffered there is little reason to ask why Acts was written. The problems arise not much with the sequel as with its predecessor, and in the area of Christology rather than in the absence of an anthropology.

The problem of distinguishing Christology from anthropology, specifically the similarity of the Jesus of Luke to the missionaries of Acts, also constitutes a major element of the theological *disunity* of Luke and Acts. The earthly Jesus is a human being, admittedly extraordinary. By virtue of his exaltation the Spirit that endowed him became available to all. This shift marks the fundamental demarcation and necessitates two separate volumes. Behind this lies the universal early Christian understanding of the exaltation of Jesus as the eschatological turning point. Lukas seeks to clarify and explicate this in two non-apocalyptic ways: via salvation history, thereby establishing historical continuity; and via anthropology, thereby demonstrating natural continuity.

Probes of such themes as eschatology, soteriology, and ethics have not yielded a unified picture. Eschatology appears to be a theme of Peter's Jerusalem sermons and drops out of the picture as the central conflict with the Jewish authorities and the concomitant gentile mission begins to develop. The death of Jesus does not have a particular saving significance in Acts.

[123] The views presented here are congruent with the "Benefactor" model of Lukan Christology developed by F. Danker in a number of writings and enhance its theoretical profile.

The text rejoices in converts of high degree, and only one representative of the mighty is cast down from his throne. There are theological themes and threads that extend through Luke and Acts, but to speak of a monolithic theological unity would be an exaggeration.[124] Most investigations assign priority to Luke and then attempt to show how Acts conforms. A possibly more fruitful line of inquiry, certainly one that would serve as a useful counter-balance, would identify the Lukan theological core in Acts and then show how this is applied, even if without complete success, to the Gospel. The foregoing chapter has thus sought to present an example of different approaches to exploring the theological unity of Luke and Acts.

[124] The "creator" of Luke-Acts, H. J. Cadbury, did not overlook theological differences between the two books (*Making*, 274–296).

5

Conclusion

H. J. Cadbury assumed, and sought to demonstrate, that Luke and Acts should be read as a unity. His theory received limited application until redaction criticism, which returned scholarly attention to the actual text of the narrative books of the New Testament, planted the seeds of literary criticism, with its concomitant focus upon these texts as narrative wholes. If the results of Cadbury's own sowing bore only thirty-fold during its first half-century, the yield since 1975 has approached one hundred. We therefore deemed it timely to subject this idea to a thorough scrutiny, not with the intention of either canonizing or deposing the prevalent view, but of providing it with suitable nuance. When unity is wholistically and indiscriminately assumed, important questions are begged and some results will be called into question. The major result of this study has been to reinforce this fundamental axiom.

The first task was the dissection of this presumed unity into several types: authorial, canonical, generic, narrative, and theological, each of which bears different implications and requires the application of particular methods. This identification, in turn, required another enterprise: the independent examination of these several types, with the object of evaluating the intrinsic probability and utility of each. A summary of our findings follows.

AUTHORIAL UNITY

The authorial unity of Luke and Acts (which is to be distinguished from identification of the author), has rarely been challenged, and we find no grounds for attempting to reopen this question. At the same time resolution of this basic issue does not determine that the same author could not have written in different genres, employed different theological constructs in the two volumes, or used different narrators. The evidence to the contrary is decisive.[1]

CANONICAL UNITY

The canonical question exposes the difficulties canons create for historical (and literary) criticism. Inclusion within a canon promotes isolation. Originally disparate works are interpreted against one another, and scholarship develops tools that, intentionally or not, foster this isolation.[2] On the ideological level the old tag "*Scriptura Scripturam interpretatur*" (Scripture interprets Scripture) remains at least covertly operative in those circles that give highly privileged status to intracanonical evidence.[3] Critical scholarship rejects the view that the Christian canon is a seamless robe, but may be prepared to view Luke-Acts as a single garment viciously rent (or accidentally divided) by the process of canonization. Canonical disunity is, from this critical perspective, a problem scholars must resolve.

[1] Josephus, who has often served as a basis of comparison with Lukas, is an example of an author who made use of different genres, ideologies, and narrative methods in his several works. See the further discussion about Josephus and Lukas in chapter 3.

[2] Examples of such tools are lexica and concordances for the OT and NT. The phenomenon is by no means limited to the biblical canon. Similar procedures affect such texts as the "Old Testament Pseudepigrapha," "The New Testament Apocrypha," the Dead Sea Scrolls, and many ancient and more recent collections.

[3] The canon is usually viewed, for these purposes, as comprised of the Hebrew Bible and twenty-seven NT books.

Comparison with the Pauline corpus is interesting. In that instance scholarship tends, with a great deal of unanimity, toward separation. Each text must be extracted from its place in the collection and independently assessed in terms of its reconstructed original situation. Scholars have for centuries stressed the particularity of each letter. Those seeking answers to questions of authenticity, integrity, the life of Paul, and the nature (and, for some, development) of Pauline thought have usually regarded the corpus as an obstacle. Only by taking the clock apart can one learn how it works and/or repair it. Yet attempts to reassemble the timepiece quite often approximate efforts to put toothpaste back into the tube. This method is open to partial challenge, particularly when Deutero-Pauline theology is viewed as integral to the formation of a corpus of Pauline letters.[4]

If separation is the norm in the case of Paul, Lukan research is wont to move in the opposite direction: toward reunification. Only by putting the clock parts back together can one make it display the correct time. At present some of the components are still lying on the table. Others have been bent here or trimmed there, and there is disagreement about the hour indicated. In each case the object is worthy: the best approximation possible of the original situation. Always, however, there is the danger of forgetting that all of these necessary endeavors are hypotheses. The varieties of critical theories advanced during the past two centuries indicate that even the proposition that Paul wrote any letters is a hypothesis.[5] The unity or unities of Luke and Acts are also hypotheses, as is the view that canonical placement is a misleading indicator of meaning. No extant manuscript or list juxtaposes Luke and Acts. The original unity of the work remains no more than a modern theory, however probable it may be.[6] The history of the formation of the New

---

[4] See H. Koester, *Introduction,* 2:261–308.

[5] This is a hypothesis to which Acts, for example, lends no support. On this subject see below, p. 000.

[6] The sequential prefaces do not prove that the works were issued at the

Testament canon does, however, reveal that early interpreters of these books did not perceive them as a unity. This evidence is certainly not decisive, but it should not be utterly neglected.

The standard canonical location of Acts, which did not become secure until the Middle Ages, already shows the head of Janus. On the one hand, it may be regarded as a sequel to the (four-fold) Gospel. On the other, it constitutes a preface to the Epistles.[7] Liturgical usage and book production indicate that the latter understanding was preferred.[8]

The canonical tug of war between Gospels and Epistles is yet another indicator that the problem of the unity of Luke and Acts is largely a problem of the classification and analysis of Acts. If, nonetheless, the two books are to be understood apart from these later arrangements, it is appropriate to examine this autonomous two-volume entity as a "canon" of sorts. Did Lukas envision them as a kind of "law" and "prophets"?[9] Or would it be better to ask if Lukas intended to produce a "Gospel" and "Apostle(s)," anticipating, perhaps inspiring, Marcion? If the Gospel were to extinguish rivals,[10] was the second volume also designed to supersede other texts? Source material existed, including stories about Stephen, Philip, Peter, and Paul. At this

---

same time or place. Luke is no less complete than Matthew. The reader of Acts would learn of a former work, but could, so to speak, manage without it.

[7] This all works rather well. John 21 ends with the risen Jesus and the disciples at breakfast. Peter is rehabilitated and given a pastoral role, enjoying a parity of sorts with the Beloved Disciple. Acts begins with the risen Jesus at table with his disciples. Peter's leadership soon emerges. There is no conflict among the apostles. As the book ends, Paul is laboring in Rome. On the next page begins Paul's letter to the Romans. It is not likely, however, that many would have been able to observe these links prior to Gutenberg.

[8] Liturgical use doubtless shaped book production. Liturgically Acts was read during the Patristic era as an Epistle on the weekdays of Easter, a practice that still obtains. On the Sundays of Eastertide, readings from Acts supplanted the OT lections. The practice was not new when Chrysostom offered his homilies on Acts.

[9] Lukan terminology fluctuates. All of the LXX may be characterized as prophecy. Luke 24:44 appears to reflect a three-fold division of Scripture, but, on the whole, the two-fold division of Law and Prophets appears to be standard (Luke 24:27; Acts 24:14; 28:23; cf. Acts 13:15).

[10] Luke 1:1-4.

juncture the Epistles rear their heads[11] to announce that the enterprise cannot be conducted apart from the study of early church history.

Frustration with scholarly deadlocks and blind alleys, often reinforced by distaste for ecclesiastically inspired conflict, has enhanced the attraction of the unified Luke and Acts as an isolated object of study. Such investigations do make assumptions about early Christian history. When they are unstated and implicit, they may contaminate the results, particularly if the implicit understanding of early church history is derived, with some or many reservations, from the portrait of Acts. It is at this level that the failure of the textual and canonical history of the New Testament documents to support the unity of Luke and Acts is most important, for that history challenges any claims that these books are to be examined in a vacuum.

GENERIC UNITY

Avoidance of examinations *in vacuo* is a specific object of form criticism. While some of those engaged in the study of Luke and Acts leave to one side the question of genre, others have in recent years attempted to find for the unified work a place among ancient literary types. The goal of this task is not — or should not be — the identification of a label that will establish sufficient unity to permit literary study, for such study does not require generic unity. In traditional terms the purpose of form criticism is to illuminate the function and purpose of a work. Literary study often seeks to illuminate the authorial audience, viewing

---

[11] Only a few scholars propose that Lukas used Pauline letters. The position most often stated is that Acts was written before collections circulated. Even if this is correct, the problem of Paul's fame as a writer of letters remains. Historically Luke and Acts fit most comfortably in the post-Pauline milieu and thus in the orbit of Deutero-Paulinism. The focus of Acts upon Ephesus indicates at the very least a Lukan interest in the metropolitan matrix of post-Pauline composition and further reduces the probability that Lukas did not know of the Epistles.

form criticism as one technique for drawing the silhouette of the implied reader.

There is nothing vaguely resembling a consensus about the single genre of Luke and Acts. Because of the work's nature, style, theme, and scope it is possible to speak only in terms of analogies, with frequent appreciation for the merits of considering a number of forms. The Lukan corpus utilizes some conventions of Greek literature and must therefore be associated with species of Greek prose, yet it also displays thorough familiarity with the language of the Greek Bible and requires examination in the light of biblical texts and forms.

Statements of unity notwithstanding, inquiries into the genre of Luke and Acts tend to give priority to one book or the other. If the Gospel has primacy, the search will turn toward biography. The single sustained effort in this direction, C. Talbert's *Literary Patterns* has failed to carry the day. Most investigations look rather toward historiography. These tend to concentrate upon Acts.[12] The problem is fundamental: Luke is a biography of some sort or another; Acts, while including biographical elements, is *not* a biography. Efforts toward identifying generic unity display tendencies to promote generic differences. At their worst (and possibly least significant) level these studies simply beg the question of generic unity. The quest for one genre that will comprehend Luke and Acts has brought many helpful insights to light and should not be abandoned. The assumption that all generic investigation must limit itself to one genre for the two does not, however, seem desirable.

NARRATIVE UNITY

The danger of *petitio principii* is even more acute in the study of narrative unity than in generic analyses. None of the studies

---

[12] This is most apparent in the articles of D. Balch ("Acts and Hellenistic Historiography") and G. Sterling ("Historiography") discussed above. Even Conzelmann's pointer toward the historical monograph, fruitfully pursued by Plümacher, takes its departure from Acts rather than Luke.

devoted to particular Gospels as narrative texts have failed to discover narrative unity.[13] Luke and Acts provide no exception, witness Tannehill's comprehensive and well-received *Narrative Unity*. The effort to reject the privileged positions of fragmenting approaches, including source, form, and redaction criticism in order to seek to make sense of the whole text as it exists is laudable, but it is not absolute.[14]

Ancient evangelists were not modern novelists. The authors of Matthew, Mark, Luke-Acts, and John worked under technical, cultural, and theological constraints that require serious attention. The presumption that they were sovereign rulers over all their material constitutes a dubious hypothesis. Most of the methods listed above were refined by New Testament scholars to deal with just these constraints, and they should retain sufficient authority to caution against expectations of immaculate unity. When dealing with Luke-Acts, it is particularly inappropriate to lash out at speculative dissections of the text, since the very subject of Luke-Acts is a modern hypothetical construct.

The literary unities of Luke and Acts are well established, as are some disunities. With the exception of the brief prefaces and the notorious "We-passages" of Acts, an anonymous, omniscient, reliable narrator speaks in both volumes. The story is sequential, with many observable, although not overt,[15] allusions to Luke that reveal correspondences between the two books. These provide the work with coherence and thematic symmetry

---

[13] Note the comments of H. Räisänen, *Messianic Secret*, 14–37. Although his strictures are too severe, limited to Mark alone, and show some lack of appreciation for the objectives of narrative analysis, his objections merit consideration. See the challenge to the presumed narrative unity of the Gospels in Moore, "Are the Gospels Unified Narratives?"

[14] But here textual criticism intrudes. The text printed in Nestle-Aland is, of course, a modern reconstruction, found in no single ancient witness. Narrative study begins with an insecure text. For an integration of textual and narrative criticism, see Parsons, *Departure*. With regard to the Fourth Gospel the narrative critic must determine whether to incorporate John 21 (and other suspect passages). If these are included, the text to be analyzed is that of the final editor and any narrative unity discovered will be secondary to that of the "original" Gospel. On this subject, see R. Culpepper, *Anatomy*.

[15] After the preface there is no more explicit reference to the first book.

but are not necessary for its understanding. The structure of Luke and Acts reveals the hand of a narrator who can impose an artistic design upon his work. By modern standards this kind of narrative design is appropriate to fiction.[16]

Is it appropriate to identify a single narrator for Luke and Acts or can one best explain the differences by positing a different narrator for each? The narrator of Acts, to follow the second model, likes the Pharisees more than did the narrator of Luke, for example, and chose a more detailed account of the Ascension, despite its earlier use. Both narrators make use of discrete episodes, but the narrator of Acts turns more often to this technique. That narrator also prefers speeches that conform more fully to the patterns of Greco-Roman rhetoric than does the narrator of Luke. While the narrator of Luke has read, so to speak, his Bible and favors sayings and parables, the narrator of Acts has also assimilated, so to speak, his Livy and shows a fondness for lengthy, interconnected dramatic episodes with set speeches at suitable points.[17] And so on. It is thus difficult to speak of an absolute rift. What the narrators share in viewpoint, technique, and style is more substantial than what they do not share,[18] but, if the notion of a narrator for each book appears too *fin*, it is serviceable at the very least in emphasizing the need to explain differences in narrative technique. At the level of discourse the narrative unity of Luke and Acts is less than perfect.

At the story level unity is not completely self-evident. Each work can stand on its own and has long done so. Rarely does one find the two books treated as full and equal elements of one whole. Those who turn to a standard New Testament hand-

---

[16] In the present era any work dominated by an omniscient narrator who shows the ultimate triumph of justice and allots vindication to the righteous reads like a novel. Interpreters and proclaimers may balk at this statement. The alternative is to concede that God seems to have lost interest in tidy plots, with all of the consequences of that view for faith and life as well as the obstacles it erects against reading the Bible. See MacQueen, *Myth,* ix–xi.

[17] One may compare the narrator of Xenophon's *Memorabilia* to the Gospel narrator, and the narrator of the *Cyropaideia* (or *Hellenica*) to the narrator of Acts.

[18] If this were not so, numerous challenges to the authorial unity of the two books would have arisen.

book do not expect to read that Luke-Acts is an Acts of Paul with an extended introduction.[19] To put it bluntly, Luke-Acts is a Gospel plus, the story of Jesus followed immediately by the story of the early Church. These stories are connected, to be sure, often ingeniously, but they are also distinguished by Lukan narrative devices and themes. The explanation of the differences that has dominated the discussion for forty years is the much-disputed thesis of the late Hans Conzelmann, who understood the differences as the literary expression of a theological attempt to correlate Christian origins with salvation history. The Gospel required a sequel to make these connections patent. Salvation history repeats itself because God is both consistent and in control.

Acts does not continue the story of Jesus, whose departure makes its story possible. It is thus best understood as a sequel rather than a second chapter or simple continuation. Luke does not leave the reader frustrated or in suspense, for it concludes where it began[20] and with the earthly career of Jesus finished. Luke and Acts do exhibit various elements of literary and narrative unity, but the assertion that they *are* a narrative unity requires refinement. On the levels of both discourse and story there are differences between the two, and narrative analyses of these texts will profit from consideration of both.[21]

THEOLOGICAL UNITY

There is little doubt that the theological unity of Luke and Acts is a good idea. Few would attempt today to construct a theology of one work quite apart from the other. The difficulty is procedural. Lukan theology proper arose with redaction

[19] As a statement of the work's interest this would not be a hopelessly defective characterization.

[20] Luke opens and closes in the Temple, creating an inclusion, a popular device in antiquity for marking literary boundaries.

[21] The best indirect witness to these differences is Robert Tannehill's *Narrative Unity of Luke-Acts*. See chapter 3, p. 48.

criticism. Application of this technique to Acts is difficult, since its speeches, which are generally held to be Lukan compositions, have been the lodes most thoroughly mined for theological data. With regard to theological investigation Lukan research has also tended toward viewing the work as a Gospel plus and the Gospel as the primary source for theology. Such subjects as eschatology, ethics, and atonement have therefore played the leading roles in the debate.

Discontent with the overdevelopment of redaction criticism has inspired some more recent scholars toward the history of religions, especially the historical and prophetic writings of the Greek Bible.[22] They thus build upon Conzelmann's categories but do so positively. For Conzelmann, Lukas's employment of salvation history was a betrayal of the Gospel. Others are less censorious and point to prophetic (specifically Deuteronomic) features to mitigate Conzelmann's characterization of Lukas as a triumphalist.[23] Informative as such studies are, they tend to give Acts short shrift and to neglect the Greco-Roman milieu, including the situation of the authorial audience.[24]

If redaction criticism is no longer monarch of methods, analysis of the speeches of Acts requires more careful attention to their narrative contexts, and not only when (as notoriously with the Areopagus Address) such attention permits setting aside the content of the speech. Tannehill has done this with some consistency, often interpreting the speeches in order to mitigate the effect of the narrative.[25]

A valid quest for the theology of Luke and Acts must begin with a statement of the primary problem addressed by these

[22] So, in particular, Tiede and Moessner.
[23] Tannehill joins in this repudiation.
[24] F. Danker, who appreciates insights derived from the LXX, has identified another model: the role of the benefactor in Mediterranean society, which permits the elucidation of Luke and Acts in terms known to almost every member of society, in particular urban society.
[25] This is most apparent on the controversial subject of Lukan attitudes toward the Jews. By seeking to find in the speeches evidence that the door remains open to Jews, Tannehill tries to qualify, sometimes to eliminate, the often hostile narrative depiction of their actions.

books and conclude with an identification of Lukas's thesis. The problem is clear enough, for the existence of two books proclaims it on the hilltops: it is the relation between Jesus' proclamation of God's reign and the Church's gospel about Jesus. The topics are Christology and ecclesiology.

Baldly stated, the difficulty with Lukan Christology involves a basic shift: the Christology of Luke is superseded by the resurrection, more or less, and becomes in turn the property of Paul and the apostles. Christology gives way to anthropology in our probe of one central theme in Lukan theology. Lukas uses elements of a common Greco-Roman anthropology as a means for forging unity between God and humankind, the histories of Israel, Jesus, and the Church, and thus between Jews and Gentiles. His object is to show the continuity of revelation and thus validate the claim of (mostly) gentile churches to share in the promises of God.

The Gospels of Matthew, Mark, and John address ecclesiological and other topics anachronistically by placing them in the life of Jesus. Through this device those evangelists bridged (and confounded) the gap between the proclaimer and the proclaimed. In theory, Lukas need not have followed this procedure. In fact, he did. This places burdens upon any who would find in Acts the necessary complement to at least some aspects of Lukan theology. Theological unity, insofar as it exists, does not support narrative unity but subverts it.

The same observation underscores Lukas's dependence upon the developing gospel genre and gives additional weight to the principle that, where theological differences between Luke and Acts exist, the latter book will normally provide the best basis for discovering distinctive features of Lukan theology.

Lukan theology has been emerging from the cloud of post-Bultmannian criticism, characterized by the epithet "theology of glory." Refutation has played a large role in this recovery. Another tack, which will have the merit of fastening upon the particularity of Lukan theology, is to characterize this dimension of Lukan thought in a non-polemical, but not uncritical, fashion. Since Lukas was not fully independent of tradition, apparently worked in an environment replete with competing theological understandings, and was more of a popular (certainly not a systematic) theologian, some inconsistency in theological expression ought not come as a surprise. Pursuit of the theological unity of Luke and Acts remains a good idea. The task itself remains outstanding, but by no means ignored.

ENVOI

According to a famous aphorism Henry J. Cadbury got a doctorate by depriving Luke of his. Do Parsons and Pervo seek fleeting fame by bursting into the domicile of this gentle man to despoil him of his precious hyphen? This book has not been a lesson in punctuation, but an effort at refinement. Acceptance of the authorial unity of Luke and Acts should not imply acceptance of unity on other levels. All types of unity are hypotheses rather than assured results. The canonical disunity deserves a bit more than curt dismissal. Luke and Acts *may* belong to one genre, but the explorations of separate genres have thus far yielded interesting data and should not be excluded. As narratives they are independent yet interrelated works. Theological unity ought not be a brush with which to efface particularity.

If Acts is to receive its due, it must be regarded as something more than an extension of Luke. Just as Luke is complete in and of itself, so is Acts. The relationships between these two books are relations *between two books*, not correspondences within a conveniently divided entirety. Literarily, Acts is best characterized as a sequel. This designation most accurately describes the reception and reading of the book from the earliest times and permits exploration of both similarities and differences within and between the works. "Luke and Acts" is therefore a more accurate designation of the relationship these books have to each other.

To H. J. Cadbury hyphenated words were like bon-bons with pebbles inside. His coinage of "Luke-Acts" was an endeavor to give each volume its due, an invitation to take up the hyphen and follow Lukas from beginning to end. Because a number of the assumptions about the unity of Luke and Acts have resulted in subordinating one book to the other or blocking off possibly promising avenues of research, we propose that Cadbury's long-suffering hyphen be awarded some times of refreshment and be spelled, at least now and then, by a far from superfluous "and."

Bibliography

Adkins, A. W. H. *From the Many to the One*. London: Constable, 1970.

Aland, K. *The Text of the New Testament: An Introduction to the Critical Editions and to the Theory and Practice of Modern Textual Criticism*, trans. E. F. Rhodes. Grand Rapids: Eerdmans, 1987.

Aune, D. *The New Testament in its Literary Environment*. LEC 8. Philadelphia: Westminster Press, 1987.

Baker, D. A. "Form and the Gospels." *Downside Review* 88 (1970): 13–26.

Balch, D. "Acts as Hellenistic Historiography." In SBLSP 24, 429–432. Atlanta: Scholars Press, 1985.

———. "The Areopagus Speech." In *Greeks, Romans, and Christians: Essays in Honor of Abraham J. Malherbe*, ed. D. Balch, E. Ferguson, and W. A. Meeks, 52–79. Minneapolis: Fortress Press, 1990.

———. "Comments on the Genre and a Political Theme of Luke-Acts: A Preliminary Comparison of Two Hellenistic Historians." In SBLSP 28, 343–361. Atlanta: Scholars Press, 1989.

Baldry, H. C. *The Unity of Mankind in Greek Thought*. Cambridge: Cambridge University Press, 1965.

Barrett, C. K. *Luke the Historian in Recent Study*. Facet Books, Biblical Series 24. Philadelphia: Fortress Press, 1970.

Benoit, P. "Some Notes on the 'Summaries' in Acts 2, 4, and 5." In *Jesus and the Gospel*, 2:95–103. New York: Herder, 1974.

Berger, K. "Hellenistische Gattungen im Neuen Testament." *Aufstieg und Niedergang der römischen Welt* II.25.2, 131–1432, 1831–1885. Berlin: Walter de Gruyter, 1984.

Betz, H. D. *Galatians*. Hermeneia. Philadelphia: Fortress Press, 1979.

———. "Gottmensch II." *Reallexikon für Antike und Christentum*. 11:234–312.

———, ed., *Plutarch's Ethical Writings and Early Christian Literature*. Studia ad Corpus Hellenisticum Novi Testamenti 3, 4. Leiden: Brill, 1975.

Blass, F. *Acta Apostolorum sive Luca ad Theophilum liberalter: Editio philologica.* Göttingen: Vandenhoeck & Ruprecht, 1895.

Booth, W. *The Rhetoric of Fiction.* Chicago: University Press, 1961.

Bovon, F. *Luke the Theologian. Thirty-Three Years of Research,* trans. K. McKinney. PTMS 12. Allison Park, PA: Pickwick Publications, 1987.

Brodie, T. L. "Greco-Roman Imitation of Texts as a Partial Guide to Luke's Use of Sources." In *Luke-Acts: New Perspectives from the Society of Biblical Literature Seminar,* ed. C. H. Talbert, 17–46. New York: Crossroad, 1984.

Brown, P. *The Body and Society: Men, Women, and Sexual Renunciation in Early Christianity.* New York: Columbia University Press, 1988.

Brown, R. "Jesus and Elisha." *Perspectives in Religious Studies* 12 (1971): 85–104.

———. *The Birth of the Messiah. A Commentary on the Infancy Narratives of Matthew and Luke.* Garden City, N.Y.: Doubleday, 1977.

Brown, S. *Apostasy and Perseverance in the Theology of Luke.* AnBib 36. Rome: Pontifical Biblical Institute, 1969.

Bruce, F. F. *The Acts of the Apostles. Greek Text with Introduction and Commentary.* 3d ed. Grand Rapids: Eerdmans, 1990.

Bultmann, R. *Theology of the New Testament,* 2 vols, trans. K. Grobel. New York: Charles Scribner's Sons, 1951–55.

Byrne, B. *'Sons of God' — 'Seed of Abraham'.* Rome: Biblical Institute Press, 1979.

Cadbury, H. J. *The Book of Acts in History.* London: A. & C. Black, 1955.

———. "Commentary on the Preface of Luke." In *The Beginnings of Christianity Part 1: The Acts of the Apostles,* Vol. II, ed. F. J. Foakes-Jackson and K. Lake, 489–510. London: Macmillan, 1922.

———. "Four Features of Lucan Style." In *Studies in Luke-Acts,* ed. L. E. Keck and J. L. Martyn, 87–102. Philadelphia: Fortress Press, 1980.

———. "Lexical Notes on Luke-Acts VI. A Proper Name for Dives." *JBL* 80 (1962): 399–402.

———. "Luke—Translator?" *AJT* 24 (1920): 436–455

———. *The Making of Luke-Acts.* London: SPCK, 1961.

———. *The Style and Literary Method of Luke. Vol. 2, The Treatment of Sources in the Gospel.* HTS 6, 83–89. Cambridge: Harvard University Press, 1920.

———. "The Summaries in Acts." In *The Beginnings of Christianity Part 1: The Acts of the Apostles.* Vol. II, ed. F. J. Foakes-Jackson and K. Lake. 392–402. London: Macmillan, 1922.

Carrington, P. *The Primitive Christian Calendar: A Study in the Making of the Marcan Gospel*. Cambridge: Cambridge University Press, 1952.

Cassidy, R. J., and P. J. Scharper, eds. *Political Issues in Luke-Acts*. Maryknoll, N.Y.: Orbis Books, 1983.

———. *Society and Politics in the Acts of the Apostles*. Maryknoll, N.Y.: Orbis Books, 1987.

Charlesworth, J. H., ed. *The Old Testament Pseudepigrapha*. 1st ed. Garden City, N.Y.: Doubleday, 1983.

Chatman, Seymour. *Story and Discourse: Narrative Structure in Fiction and Film*. Ithaca, N.Y.: Cornell University Press, 1978.

Childs, B. S. *The New Testament as Canon: An Introduction*. Philadelphia: Fortress Press, 1984.

Clark, A. C. *The Acts of the Apostles*. Oxford: The Clarendon Press, 1933.

Conzelmann, H. *Acts of the Apostles*, trans. and ed. E. J. Epp with C. Matthews. Hermeneia. Philadelphia: Fortress Press, 1987.

———. *The Theology of St. Luke*, 1960, trans. G. Buswell. Reprint. Philadelphia: Fortress Press, 1982.

Culpepper, R. A. *Anatomy of the Fourth Gospel. A Study in Literary Design*. Philadelphia: Fortress Press, 1983.

———. "Commentary on Biblical Narratives: Changing Paradigms." *Foundations & Facets Forum* 5 (1989): 87–102.

Dalbert, P. *Die Theologie der hellenistisch-jüdischen Missionsliteratur unter Ausschluss von Philo u. Josephus*. TF 4. Hamburg-Volksdorf: H. Reich, 1954.

Danker, F. *Jesus and the New Age. A Commentary on St. Luke's Gospel*. Rev. ed. Philadelphia: Fortress Press, 1988.

———. "Review." *JBL* 106 (1987): 143–144.

Davies, J. G. "The Prefigurement of the Ascension in the Third Gospel." *JTS* 6 (1955): 229–230.

Dawsey, James. "The Literary Unity of Luke-Acts: Questions of Style — A Task for Literary Critics." *NTS* 35 (1989): 48–66.

———. *The Lukan Voice: Confusion and Irony in the Gospel of Luke*. Macon, Ga.: Mercer University Press, 1986.

Delling, G. "Gotteskindschaft." *RAC* 11:1159–1185.

Dibelius, M. *From Tradition to Gospel*, trans. B. Woolf. New York: Charles Scribner's Sons, 1935.

———. *Studies in the Acts of the Apostles*, trans. M. Ling and P. Schubert; ed. H. Greeven. New York: Charles Scribner's Sons, 1956.

Dörrie, H. *Der Königskult des Antiochus von Kommagene im Lichte Neuer Inschriften-Funde*. Göttingen: Vandenhoeck & Ruprecht, 1964.

Drury, J. *Tradition and Design in Luke's Gospel.* Atlanta: John Knox Press, 1976.

Duplacy, J. "La préhistorie du texte in Luc 22.43-44." In *New Testament Textual Criticism: Its Significance for Exegesis: Essays in Honor of Bruce M. Metzger,* ed. E. J. Epp and G. D. Fee, 81–86. Oxford: Oxford University Press, 1981.

Dupont, J. "La Question du plan des Actes des Apôtres à la lumière d'un texte du Lucien de Samosate." *NovT* 21 (1979): 220-231.

Egger, B. "Women in the Greek Novel: Constructing the Feminine." Diss. University of California, Irvine, 1990.

Ehrman, B. D. and Plunkett, M. A. "The Angel and the Agony: The Textual Problem of Luke 22:43-44." *CBQ* 45 (1983): 401-416.

Esler, P. *Community and Gospel in Luke-Acts. The Social and Political Motivations of Lucan Theology.* Cambridge: Cambridge University Press, 1987.

Ferguson, J. *Utopias of the Classical World.* London: Thames & Hudson, 1975.

Fitzmyer, J. "The Ascension of Christ and Pentecost." *TS* 45 (1984): 409-440.

———. *Luke the Theologian: Aspects of His Teaching.* Mahwah, N.J.: Paulist Press, 1989.

———. *The Gospel according to Luke.* 2 vols. AB 28-28A. Garden City, N.Y.: Doubleday, 1981-85.

Fornara, C. W. *The Nature of History in Ancient Greece and Rome.* Berkeley: University of California Press, 1983.

Fowler, R. M. *Loaves and Fishes: The Function of the Feeding Stories in the Gospel of Mark.* SBLDS 54. Chico, Calif.: Scholars Press, 1981.

Fox, R. L. *Pagans and Christians.* New York: Knopf, 1987.

Funk, R. W. *The Poetics of Biblical Narrative.* Sonoma, Calif.: Polebridge Press, 1988.

Gamble, H. "The Canon of the New Testament." In *The New Testament and Its Modern Interpreters,* ed. E. J. Epp and G. W. MacRae, 201-243. Philadelphia: Fortress Press; Atlanta: Scholars Press, 1989.

Garrett, S. *The Demise of the Devil. Magic and the Demonic in Luke's Writings.* Minneapolis: Fortress Press, 1989.

Gasque, W. W. *A History of the Criticism of the Acts of the Apostles.* Peabody, Mass.: Hendrickson, 1989.

Gaventa, B. R. "The Peril of Modernizing Henry Joel Cadbury." In *Cadbury, Knox, and Talbert: American Contributions to the Study of Acts,* ed. M. C. Parsons and J. B. Tyson, 7-26. Atlanta: Scholars Press, 1992.

Geldenhuys, J. N. *Commentary on the Gospel of Luke.* Grand Rapids: Eerdmans, 1952.

Genette, G. *Narrative Discourse: An Essay in Method,* trans. J. E. Lewin. Ithaca: Cornell University Press, 1980.

George, A. *Études sur l'oeuvre de Luc.* Paris: Gabalda, 1978.

Georgi, D. *The Opponents of Paul in Second Corinthians.* Philadelphia: Fortress Press, 1985.

Goodspeed, E. J. "The Origin of Acts." *JBL* 39 (1920): 83–101.

Goulder, M. D. *Luke: A New Paradigm.* Sheffield: JSOT Press, 1989.

———. *Midrash and Lection in Matthew.* London: SPCK, 1974.

———. *The Evangelists' Calendar: A Lectionary Explanation of the Development of Scripture.* London: SPCK, 1978.

Gowler, D. B. *Host, Guest, Enemy, and Friend. Portraits of the Pharisees in Luke and Acts.* New York: Peter Lang, 1991.

Grant, R. McL. *Miracle and Natural Law.* Amsterdam: North Holland Pub. Co., 1952.

Grundmann, W. "δύναμαι, κ.τ.λ.," *TDNT* 2:284–317.

Haenchen, E. *The Acts of the Apostles,* trans. R. McL. Wilson *et al.* Philadelphia: Westminster Press, 1971.

Hawkins, J. C. *Horae Synopticae. Contributions to the Study of the Synoptic Problem.* 2d ed. Oxford: Clarendon Press, 1907.

Hedrick, C. W. "Authorial Presence and Narrator in John: Commentary and Story." In *Gospel Origins and Christian Beginnings in Honor of James M. Robinson,* ed. J. E. Goehring, C. W. Hedrick, and J. T. Sanders, 74–93. Sonoma, Calif.: Polebridge Press, 1990.

———, "Narrator and Story in the Gospel of Mark: *Hermeneia* and *Paradosis,*" *Perspectives in Religious Studies* 14 (1987): 239–258.

Hemer, C. J. *The Book of Acts in the Setting of Hellenistic History.* Tübingen: J. C. B. Mohr, 1989.

Hengel, M. *Acts and the History of Earliest Christianity,* trans. J. Bowden. Philadelphia: Fortress Press, 1979.

Holliday, C. *Fragments From Hellenistic Jewish Authors, Vol. 1: Historians.* SBLTT 20. Chico, Calif.: Scholars Press, 1983.

Jervell, J. *Imago Dei. Gen 1:26f. im Spätjudentum, in der Gnosis und in den paulinischen Briefen.* Göttingen: Vandenhoeck & Reprecht, 1960.

———. *Luke and the People of God: A New Look at Luke-Acts.* Minneapolis: Augsburg Publishing House, 1972.

Johnson, L. T. "On Finding the Lukan Community: A Cautious Cautionary Essay." SBLSP 18, 87–100. Missoula, Mont.: Scholars Press, 1979.

——. *The Literary Function of Possessions in Luke-Acts.* Chico, Calif.: Scholars Press, 1977.

Jones, D. L. "The Legacy of Henry Joel Cadbury: Or What Cadbury Learned That We Ought to Know." In *Cadbury, Knox, and Talbert: American Contributions to the Study of Acts,* ed. M. C. Parsons and J. B. Tyson. Atlanta: Scholars Press, 1992.

Juel, D. *Luke-Acts: The Promise of History.* Atlanta: John Knox Press, 1983.

Kloppenborg, J. S. *The Formation of Q.* Philadelphia: Fortress Press, 1987.

Knox, W. L. *The Acts of the Apostles.* Cambridge: Cambridge University Press, 1948.

Koester, H. *Introduction to the New Testament,* 2 vols. Berlin and New York: Walter de Gruyter, 1982.

——. "φύσις, κ.τ.λ.," *TDNT* 9:251–277.

Krodel, G. *Acts.* Augsburg Commentary. Minneapolis: Augsburg Publishing House, 1986.

Kurz, W. S. "Hellenistic Rhetoric in the Christological Proof of Luke-Acts." *CBQ* 42 (1980): 171–195.

——. "Narrative Approaches to Luke-Acts." *Bib* 68 (1987): 195–220.

——. "Luke 3:23-38 and Greco-Roman and Biblical Genealogies." In *Luke-Acts: New Perspectives from the Society of Biblical Literature Seminar,* ed. C. Talbert, 169–187. New York: Crossroad, 1984.

——. "Narrative Models for Imitation in Luke-Acts." In *Greeks, Romans, and Christians: Essays in Honor of Abraham J. Malherbe,* ed. D. Balch, E. Ferguson, W. Meeks, 171–189. Minneapolis, Fortress Press, 1990.

Lake, K. and F. J. Foakes-Jackson D.D., eds. *The Acts of the Apostles,* 5 vols. London: Macmillan, 1920–33.

Lanser, S. S. *The Narrative Act: Point of View in Prose Fiction.* Princeton: Princeton University Press, 1981.

Leaney, A. R. C. *A Commentary on the Gospel of Luke.* 2d ed. London: Black, 1966.

Levinsohn, S. *Textual Connections in Acts.* Atlanta: Scholars Press, 1987.

——. "Notes on the Distribution of *de* and *kai* in the Narrative Framework of Luke's Gospel." In *Selected Technical Articles Related to Translation* 5 (1981): 39–53.

Levinson, J. R. *Portraits of Adam in Early Judaism.* JSPSup 1. Sheffield: JSOT Press, 1988.

Lutz, C. E. *Musonius Rufus. "The Roman Socrates."* New Haven: Yale University Press, 1947.

Mackay, B. S. "Plutarch and the Miraculous." In *Miracles,* ed. C. F. D. Moule, 97–115. London: Mowbray, 1965.

MacQueen, B. D. *Myth, Rhetoric, and Fiction. A Reading of Longus's Daphnis and Chloe.* Lincoln: University of Nebraska Press, 1990.

Maddox, R. *The Purpose of Luke-Acts.* Edinburgh: T. & T. Clark, 1982.

Malherbe, A., *Paul and the Popular Philosophers.* Minneapolis: Fortress Press, 1989.

Marshall, I. H. *The Gospel of Luke: A Commentary on the Greek Text.* Grand Rapids: Eerdmans, 1978.

Menoud, P. H. "Pendant quarante jours (Actes 1:3)." In *Neotestamentica et patristica: Eine Freundesgabe, Herrn Professor Dr. Oscar Cullmann zu seinem 60. Geburtstag überreicht,* 148–156. NovTSup 6. Leiden: Brill, 1962.

Metzger, B. *A Textual Commentary on the Greek New Testament,* 3d ed. London: United Bible Societies, 1975.

Michaelis, W. "μιμέομαι, κ.τ.λ.," *TDNT* 4:659–674.

———. "ὁμοιοπαθῆς," *TDNT* 5:938–939.

Minear, P. "Luke's Use of the Birth Stories." In *Studies in Luke-Acts,* ed. L. E. Keck and J. L. Martyn, 111–130. Nashville: Abingdon Press, 1966.

Moessner, D. *Lord of the Banquet.* Minneapolis: Fortress Press, 1989.

Moore, S. "Are the Gospels Unified Narratives?" In SBLSP 26, ed. K. H. Richards, 443–458. Atlanta: Scholars Press, 1987.

———. *Literary Criticism and the Gospels: The Theoretical Challenge.* New Haven: Yale University Press, 1989.

———. "Narrative Commentaries on the Bible: Context, Roots, and Prospects." *Foundations & Facets Forum* 3 (1987): 29–62.

Morris, L. "The Gospels and the Jewish Lectionaries." In *Gospel Perspectives, 3: Studies in Midrash and Historiography,* ed. R. T. France and D. Wenham, 129–156. Sheffield: JSOT Press, 1983.

Moule, C. F. D., ed. *Miracles.* London: Mowbray, 1965.

Neyrey, J. *The Passion according to Luke. A Redaction Study of Luke's Soteriology.* New York: Paulist Press, 1985.

———, ed. *The Social World of Luke-Acts.* Peabody: Hendrickson Publishers, 1991.

Nickelsburg, G. W. E. *Studies on the Testament of Joseph.* Missoula, Mont.: Scholars Press, 1975.

———. "The Genre and Function of the Markan Passion Narrative." *HTR* 73 (1980): 154–184.

Nock, A. D. *Essays on Religion and the Ancient World.* 2 vols., ed. Z. Stewart. Cambridge: Harvard University Press, 1972.

Nolland, J. *Luke 1–9:20.* Word Biblical Commentary. Dallas: Word, 1989.

O'Toole, R. *The Unity of Luke's Theology: An Analysis of Luke-Acts.* GNS 9. Wilmington, DE: Michael Glazier Press, 1984.

Parker, P. "The 'Former Treatise' and the Date of Acts." *JBL* 84 (1965): 52–58.

Parsons, M. C., "Canonical Criticism." In *New Testament Criticism and Interpretation,* ed. D. Black and D. Dockery, 279–287. Grand Rapids: Zondervan, 1991.

———. *The Departure of Jesus in Luke-Acts: The Ascension Narratives in Context.* JSNTSup 21. Sheffield: JSOT Press, 1987.

———. "Reading Talbert." In SBLSP 26. Atlanta: Scholars Press, 1987.

———. "The Unity of the Lukan Writings: Rethinking the *Opinio Communis.*" In *With Steadfast Purpose: Essays in Honor of Henry Jackson Flanders,* ed. N. H. Keathley, 29–53. Waco, Tex.: Baylor University Press, 1990.

——— and J. Tyson, eds. *Cadbury, Knox, and Talbert: American Contributions to the Study of Acts.* SBLBSNA, ed. Kent Richards. Atlanta: Scholars Press, 1992.

Pease, A. S., ed. *M. Tulli Ciceronis De Divinatione.* 2 vols. Urbana: University of Illinois Press, 1920–23.

———, ed. *M. Tulli Ciceronis De Natura Deorum.* 2 vols. Cambridge: Harvard University Press, 1955–58.

Pervo, R. *Luke's Story of Paul.* Minneapolis: Fortress Press, 1990.

———. "Must Luke and Acts Be Treated as One Genre?" In SBLSP 28, 309–16. Atlanta: Scholars Press, 1989.

———. "On Perilous Things: A Response to Beverly R. Gaventa." In *Cadbury, Knox, and Talbert: American Contributions to the Study of Acts,* eds. M. C. Parsons and J. B. Tyson. Atlanta: Scholars Press, 1992.

———. *Profit with Delight. The Literary Genre of the Acts of the Apostles.* Philadelphia: Fortress Press, 1987.

Petersen, N. "'Point of View' in Mark's Narrative." *Semeia* 12 (1978): 97–112.

Plümacher, E. "Die Apostelgeschichte als historische Monographie." In *Les Actes des Apôtres,* ed. J. Kremer, 457–466. BETL 68. Gembloux: Louvain University Press, 1979.

———. "Acta-Forschung 1974–1982." *TRu* 49 (1984): 138–153.

———. "Lukas als griechischer Historiker." *RESup* 14:235–64.

———. "Apostelgeschichte." *TRe* 1: 483–528. Berlin: Walter de Gruyter, 1978.

———. "Lukas als griechischer Schriftsteller." *RESup* 14:235–264.

——. *Lukas als hellenistischer Schriftsteller: Studien zur Apostelgeschichte.* SUNT 9. Göttingen: Vandenhoeck & Rupprecht, 1972.

——. "Monographie." In *Les Actes des apôtres.* BETL 48, ed. J. Kremer, 457–66. Louvain: Louvain University Press, 1979.

Plummer, A. *A Critical and Exegetical Commentary on the Gospel according to St. Luke.* ICC, 5th ed. Edinburgh: T. & T. Clark, 1922.

Powell, M. A. *What Are They Saying about Acts?* New York: Paulist Press, 1991.

——. *What Is Narrative Criticism?* Minneapolis: Fortress Press, 1990.

Praeder, S. M. "Jesus-Paul, Peter-Paul, and Jesus-Peter Parallelisms in Luke-Acts: A History of Reader Response." In SBLSP 23, 39. Atlanta: Scholars Press, 1984.

——. "The Problem of First Person Narration in Acts." *NovT* 29 (1987): 193–218.

Price, S. R. F. *Rituals and Power. The Roman Imperial Cult in Asia Minor.* Cambridge: Cambridge University Press, 1984.

Puskas, C. B. "The Conclusion of Luke-Acts: An Investigation of the Literary Function and Theological Significance of Acts 28:16-31." Th.D. Diss., St. Louis University, 1980.

Räisänen, H. *The 'Messianic Secret' in Mark's Gospel,* trans. C. Tuckett. Edinburgh: T. & T. Clark, 1990.

Ramsay, W. M. *St. Paul the Traveller and Roman Citizen.* New York: Macmillan, 1906.

Reardon, B. P., ed. *Collected Ancient Greek Novels.* Berkeley: University of California Press, 1989.

Reitzenstein, R. *Hellenistische Wundererzählungen.* Darmstadt: Wissenschaftliche Buchgesellschaft, 1974.

Rhoads, D. and Michie, D. *Mark as Story: An Introduction to the Narrative of a Gospel.* Philadelphia: Fortress Press, 1982.

Richard, E. "Luke—Writer, Theologian, Historian: Research and Orientation of the 1970's." *BTB* 13 (1983): 3–15.

Rimmon-Kenan, S. *Narrative Fiction: A Contemporary Poetics.* London: Methuen, 1983.

Robbins, V. K. "The Social Location of the Implied Author of Luke-Acts." In *The Social World of Luke-Acts: Models for Interpretation,* ed. J. H. Neyrey, 305–332. Peabody: Hendrickson Publishers, Inc. 1991.

Schaff, P., ed. *A Select Library of the Nicene and Post-Nicene Fathers of the Christian Church.* Vol. 11. *Saint Chrysostom: Homilies on the Acts of the Apostles and the Epistle to the Romans.* Grand Rapids: Eerdmans, 1979.

Schmidt, D. "The Historiography of Acts: Deuteronomistic or Hellenistic?" In SBLSP 24, 417–427.

Schneider, G. *Die Apostelgeschichte.* 2 vols. Freiburg: Herder & Herder, 1980–82.

Schneider, J. "ὅμοιος, κ.τ.λ.," *TDNT* 5:186–199.

Schürmann, H. *Das Lukasevangelium, Erster Teil, Kommentar zu Kap. 1.1 – 9,50.* Herders theologischer Kommentar zum Neuen Testament 3. Freiburg: Herder, 1969.

Schweizer, A. "υἱός," *TDNT* 8:363–392.

Sheeley, S. "The Narrator in the Gospel: Developing A Model." *PRS* 16 (1989): 213–223.

———. *Narrative Asides in Luke-Acts.* JSNTSup 72. Sheffield: Sheffield Academic Press, 1992.

Smith, B. H. "Narrative Versions, Narrative Theories." *Critical Inquiry* 7 (1980): 213–236.

Smith, R. H. "The Theology of Acts." *CTM* 42 (1971): 527–535.

Souter, A. *The Text and Canon of the New Testament.* New York: Charles Scribner's Sons, 1913.

Speyer, W. "Genealogie." *RAC* 9:1145–1267. Stuttgart: Hirsemann, 1950.

Stagg, F. "The Journey Toward Jerusalem in Luke's Gospel." *RevExp* 64 (1967): 499–512.

Staley, J. L. *The Print's First Kiss: A Rhetorical Investigation of the Implied Reader in the Fourth Gospel.* SBLDS 82. Atlanta: Scholars Press, 1988.

Stanley, D. M. *Jesus in Gethsemene: The Early Church Reflects on the Suffering of Jesus,* 205–217. New York: Paulist Press, 1980.

Steichele, H. "Vergleich der Apostelgeschichte mit der antiken Geschichtsschreibung." Ph.D. Diss., University of Munich, 1971.

Sterling, G. E. *Historiography and Self-Definition: Josephus, Luke-Acts and Apologetic Historiography.* NovTSup 64. Leiden: Brill, 1992.

———. "Luke-Acts and Apologetic Historiography." In SBLSP 28, 326–342.

Sternberg, M. *The Poetics of Biblical Narrative: Ideological Literature and the Drama of Reading.* Indiana Literary Biblical Series. Bloomington, Ind.: Indiana University Press, 1985.

Stowers, S. K. "Paul on the Use and Abuse of Reason." In *Greeks, Romans, and Christians: Essays in Honor of Abraham J. Malherbe,* ed. D. Balch, E. Ferguson, and W. A. Meeks, 253–286. Minneapolis: Fortress Press, 1990.

Sundberg, A. "Canon Muratori: A Fourth Century List." *HTR* 66 (1973): 1–41.

Sweet, J. P. M. "The Theory of Miracles in the Wisdom of Solomon." In *Miracles*, ed. C. F. D. Moule, 115–126. London: Mowbray, 1965.

Talbert, C. *Literary Patterns, Theological Themes, and the Genre of Luke-Acts.* SBLMS 20. Missoula, Mont.: Scholars Press, 1974.

———, ed. *Luke-Acts. New Perspectives from the Society of Biblical Literature Seminar.* New York: Crossroad, 1984.

———. "Once Again: Gospel Genre." *Semeia* 43 (1988): 53–73.

———, ed. *Perspectives on Luke-Acts.* Edinburgh: T. & T. Clark, 1978.

———. *Reading Luke.* New York: Crossroad, 1982.

———. Review of Robert Tannehill, *The Narrative Unity of Luke-Acts: A Literary Interpretation. Vol 1: The Gospel According to Luke. Bib* 69 (1988): 135–138.

———. *What is a Gospel?* Philadelphia: Fortress Press, 1977.

Tannehill, R. *The Narrative Unity of Luke-Acts: A Literary Interpretation.* 2 vols. Philadelphia and Minneapolis: Fortress Press, 1986-1990.

Tiede, D. *Prophecy and History in Luke-Acts.* Philadelphia: Fortress Press, 1980.

Tolbert, M. A. *Sowing the Gospel. Mark's World in Literary-Historical Perspective.* Minneapolis: Fortress Press, 1989.

Torgovnick, M. *Closure in the Novel.* Princeton: Princeton University Press, 1981.

Torrey, C. C. *The Composition and Date of Acts.* HTS 1. Cambridge: Harvard University Press, 1916.

Tsirpanlis, C. N. *Introduction to Eastern Patristic Thought and Orthodox Theology.* Collegeville, Minn.: The Liturgical Press, 1992.

Turner, N. "Style." In *A Grammar of New Testament Greek*, ed. J. H. Moulton, Vol. 4. Edinburgh: T. & T. Clark, 1976.

Tyson, J. *The Death of Jesus in Luke-Acts.* Columbia: University of South Carolina Press, 1986.

Uspensky, B. *A Poetics of Composition: the Structure of the Artistic Text and Typology of a Compositional Form*, trans. V. Zavarin and S. Wittig. Berkeley: University of California Press, 1973.

Van Seters, J. *In Search of History.* New Haven: Yale University Press, 1983.

Van Unnik, W. C. "Luke-Acts, a Storm Center in Contemporary Scholarship." In *Studies in Luke-Acts*, ed. L. E. Keck and J. L. Martyn, 15–32. Philadelphia: Fortress Press, 1980.

———. "Luke's Second Book and the Rules of Hellenistic Historiography." In *Les Actes des Apôtres: Traditions, rédaction, théologie*, ed. J. Kremer, 37–60. Gembloux: Leuven University Press, 1979.

Veltmann, F. "The Defense Speeches of Paul in Acts." In *Perspectives on Luke-Acts,* ed. C. H. Talbert, 243–256. Edinburgh: T. & T. Clark, 1978.

Wall, R. "The Acts of the Apostles in Canonical Context." *BTB* 18 (1988): 15–24.

Walworth, A. J. "The Narrator of Acts." Ph.D. Diss., The Southern Baptist Theological Seminary, 1985.

Wilder, A. N. "Variant Traditions of the Resurrection in Acts." *JBL* 62 (1943): 307–318.

Wildhaber, B. *Paganisme populaire et prédication apostolique.* Geneva: Labor et Fides, 1987.

Williams, C. S. C. "The Date of Luke-Acts." *ExpTim* 64 (1953): 283–284.

Williamson, R. *Jews in the Hellenistic World. Philo.* Cambridge: Cambridge University Press, 1989.

Winston, D. *Wisdom of Solomon.* AB 43. Garden City, N.Y.: Doubleday, 1979.

Wuellner, W. "Narrative Criticism and the Lazarus Story." Unpublished paper presented to the Society for New Testament Studies, 1981.

Ancient Sources

14:1-24	37 n. 72, 68	24:27	118 n. 9
14:7	75	24:28	72
14:16-24	51	24:31	110
15:3ff	103	24:37	72
15:11-16	109 n. 106	24:38	73
15:11-32	51, 104 n. 83	24:44	118 n. 9
15:17	104 n. 83	24:47	59, 64
15:20-32	104 n. 83	24:48	59
15:27	50	24:49	59, 111 n. 118
16:19-31	51	24:50-53	10 n. 40, 11, 59, 60,
17:16	75 n. 119		62, 63
17:20-37	85 n. 5	*1 Maccabees*	34, 41
18:1	75	*2 Maccabees*	34, 41
18:14	108	*3 Maccabees*	26, 34, 99 n. 62
19:1-10	39 n. 76	*4 Maccabees*	34, 92 n. 33, 101
19:5-9	88 n. 19		n. 72
19:11	72	Manetho	32 n. 50
19:11-27	51	Mark	
19:27	68	2:1-12	95
19:29	68	5:27-31	112 n. 121
19:37	68	5:41	69
20:9-16	51	6:1-6	78
20:27	75, 76	7:22	108
20:33	76	13	85
20:35-38	101 n. 72	14:3-9	78
20:38	101 n. 72	15:33	95
21:5-36	85 n. 4	16:5	64
21:34-36	88 n. 22	16:8	64
21:37	68	16:9-20	86 n. 12
22	105 n. 86	Matthew	
22:1	75	1:23	70
22:14-38	37 n. 72	7:6	109 n. 109
22:39	105 n. 86	7:23	109 n. 108
22:39-46	105	Mishnah	41 n. 89
22:61	72	Muratorian Canon	22
23	57	Musonius Rufus	108
23:12	74	*Nemean Odes*	98 n. 55
23:18-19	75	Nicolaus of Damascus	28 n. 33
23:43	88 n. 19	Numbers 20:1-13	93 n. 37
23:44	95	Origen	28 n. 37, 94 n. 39
23:50-51	71, 75	2 Peter	66 n. 91
24	9, 59, 78	P^{45}	8
24:4	60	P^{66}	60 n. 69
24:8	72	P^{74}	9
24:13-35	110	P^{75}	60 n. 69
24:20-21	87 n. 16	Philippians 3:2	109 n. 109
24:26	87 n. 16		

Philo   63, 92 n. 33, 93 nn. 35-37,
            94 n. 41, 99, 102 n. 73,
            108 n. 102, 111 n. 115
De Abrahamo   93 n. 36
De Confusione Linguarum
            99 n. 64, 111 n. 115
De Decalogo   93 n. 35, 99
                            n. 64
Quod Deterius Potiori Insidiari
   Soleat   111 n. 115
De Opificio Mundi   108 n. 102,
                        111 n. 115
De Praemiis et Poenis   93
                            n. 35
De Somniis   108 n. 102
De Specialibus Legibus   93
            n. 35, 108 n. 102
De Vita Mosis   63, 92 n. 33,
            93 n. 37, 111 n. 115
Philostratus   107 n. 100
Plato   98 n. 56, 105 n. 90,
            107, 108 n. 105
Protagoras   98 n. 56
Republic   107 n. 98
Theatetus   105 n. 90, 108
                            n. 105
Timaeus   105 n. 90
Pliny   107 n. 100
Plutarch   99 n. 60, 107
Ei apud Delphos   107 n. 97
De Esu Carnis   107 n. 97
De Exil   99 n. 60
Moralia   107 n. 97
Polybius   28 nn. 34 and 35
Polyhistor (*See* Alexander Polyhistor)
Pompeius Trogus   28 n. 33

Posidonius   28 nn. 33 and 35
Psalms
72:22   107 n. 95
82:6   99
143:4   92 n. 33
Psalms of Solomon   101 n. 71
Revelation 22:15   109 n. 109
Seneca   98 n. 54
Sentences of Sextus   99 n. 61
Sibylline Oracles   93 n. 37, 99
            n. 62, 107 n. 100
Sirach   101 n. 71, 102 n. 73
Talmud   41 n. 89
Tertullian   21 n. 6
   Against Marcion   21 n. 6
   Prescription Against Heretics   21
                            n. 6
Testament of Abraham   102 n. 72,
                        110 n. 112
Testament of Levi   105 n. 86
Thucydides   16, 24
Timaeus   28 n. 35
Timagenes   28 n. 33
Titus
3:3   108
1:12   109 n. 109
Vergil   41
Wisdom of Solomon   92 n. 33,
            94 n. 41, 100 n. 68
Xenophon of Athens   16, 122
                            n. 17
Cyropaideia   122 n. 17
Hellenica   16, 122 n. 17
Memorabilia   122 n. 17
Xenophon of Ephesus   91 n. 30

Modern Authors